Trust Me With Your Heart Again

A Fireside Treasury of Turn-of-the-Century Sheet Music Collected by Norton Stillman

A FIRESIDE BOOK
PUBLISHED BY
SIMON AND SCHUSTER

To
Grandma Grace

A Fireside Book
Published by Simon and Schuster
Rockefeller Center, 630 Fifth Avenue
New York, New York 10020
First paperback edition 1973
SBN 671-21037-8 Casebound
SBN 671-21667-8 Paperback
Library of Congress Catalog Card Number: 70-159138
Designed by Helen Barrow
Manufactured in the United States of America

1 2 3 4 5 6 7 8 9 10

CONTENTS

Part I ROMANTIC BALLADS

Part II PATHETIC BALLADS

Part III COMIC SONGS & POPULAR NOVELTIES

PART ONE

ROMANTIC BALLADS

Musical Supplement to the SUNDAY CHRONICLE
Chicago, Sunday, April 14th 1901.

THE EYES THAT I LOVE THE BEST.

Words and Music by B. H. JANSSEN.

1. You ask me eyes I love the best, If black, or blue, or gray? I know not which I prize the most, I real-ly can-not

2. Tho' paths in life be rough and steep, What-e'er my lot may be; Tho' clouds hide ev-'ry ray of light, Those eyes I al-ways

say; .... I on - ly know they watch for me At
see; .... To me...... they tell what-e'er...... is mine, Each

noon - time and at night,............ They greet me and they
joy, or pain, or woe,............ Finds ech - o in my

say good bye, And when I come, grow bright............
loved one's heart, Wher-e'er I am, or go. ....

CHORUS.

Sad and bright are the lov - ing eyes Up at the win - dow-

mf

TILL I MET YOU, I NEVER KNEW OF LOVE, SWEET LOVE

WORDS BY
GEO. H. DIAMOND

MUSIC BY
MABEL DUDLEY HILLIARD

PUBLISHED BY
GEO. H. DIAMOND
199 3RD AVENUE, N.Y.

5

Dedicated to Mrs. Nellie Cutchin Riddick.

'Till I Met You, I Never Knew Of Love Sweet Love.

Words by
George H. Diamond.

Music by
Mabel Dudley Hilliard.

Dar-ling 'mong the pines of Maine I spent my child-hood, Where the
As so hap-pi-ly we glide in our can-noe dear, While the

pret-ty birds were sing-ing all the day,_____ Ma-ny
twi-light sha-dows steal a-cross the sky,_____ Once a-

hours I spent a-roam-ing thro' the wild-wood, 'Neath the
gain let's whis-per of our love so true dear, Of the

ni - cest girl in all this world to love.
love that's in my heart I'll give to you.

rall.

Chorus.
Sweetly

I nev-er knew the fra-grance of the blush-ing rose dear,___ I nev-er

p

felt the love-ly moon-beam's soft ca - ress,_____ I nev-er

knew the joy of liv - ing Hea - ven knows dear,___ Un - til your

TELL ME WHO YOU LOVE

BY HOWARD & EMERSON

TELL ME WHO YOU LOVE!

By Howard and Emerson.

Ans-wer it so soft-ly in ac-cents pure and clear, The
Tho' I've heard the sto-ry so oft-en o'er and o'er, I

sto-ry that my long-ing soul would hear!
long to hear it whispered just once more!

Lov-ing-ly I'll fold you to my breast;
What would be this world with-out you, dear?

One word, on-ly one from you will bring me rest! Give me your ans-wer,
Life with all its joys and splendor would be drear; You are my an-gel

rit.

all joys a - bove — Tell me, sweetheart, who you love! _____
sent from a - bove! Tell me, sweetheart, who you love! _____

rit.

REFRAIN. Andante.

Look in mine eyes, love,— soft - ly re - ply - ing,

One word—just one — for that I'm sigh - ing! Sweet, with a kiss, Oh,

an - swer me this, dear. Tell me who you love! _____

rit.

SWEET BUNCH OF DAISIES.

A
BEAUTIFUL BALLAD
WITH
WALTZ REFRAIN.
50¢

BY
ANITA OWEN.

WABASH MUSIC COMPANY,
26 VAN BUREN STREET,
CHICAGO.

Sweet Bunch of Daisies.

Waltz Song and Refrain.

Words and Music by ANITA OWEN.

1. Sweet   gold - en   dai - - sies,   Oh,   how dear   to   me,.........
2. Sweet   with - ered dai - - sies,   Treas - ured more   than   gold,.........

REFRAIN.

Sweet bunch of dai - sies,........ Brought from the dell.........

Kiss me once, dar - ling,...... Dai - - sies won't tell..........

Give me your prom - ise,...... O sweet - heart do,..........

Dar - - ling I love you,...... Will you be true?........

I'M · LONGING · FOR YOU · EVERY · DAY

·BY · H·B·BLANKE· COMPOSER OF LAZARRE

WHITNEY · WARNER · PUB·CO· DETROIT · NEW·YORK· 5

I'm Longing For You Every Day.

(BALLAD.)

H. B. BLANKE.
Composer of "Lazarre" and
"Under the Rose" Waltzes.

1. My thot's are sum-mer birds that fly
2. The sun-shine of the mer - - ry spring

To you on wings of sweet de-light!
Brings back your dear sweet face to me!

I watch the stars that
I hear you speak in

gem   the sky   And in them see your smile so   bright,
birds   that sing   A - mid the flow-ers of   the   lea,

I can-not keep you from   my heart   The ros-es whis - per
'Tis vain for me now   to   for-get   For you a-lone   I

dreams   of you: And each sad mom - ent   we're   a-part
breathe   each sigh: The sun of hope   for   me   hath set

But   makes my   love more fond   and   true.
When you're not nigh, when you're not nigh.

CHORUS.

I'm long-ing for you ev-ery day My

heart is lone while you're a-way For you are dear-er far to

me_____ Than life_ than all the world could be I'm

long-ing for you sweet-heart I'm long-ing for you ev-ery day.

rit.

MY IDEAL GIRL
NOVELTY SONG
M. WITMARK & SONS
NEW YORK · CHICAGO · SAN FRANCISCO · LONDON · PARIS · MELBOURNE

My Ideal Girl.

Words by
MAURICE E. MARKS.

Music by
ED. ROSENBAUM, Jr.

bout their sweet - hearts love - li - ness___ and of - fered my com -
some - thing catch - - es in my throat___ When I would make com -

pas - sion. But some - thing strange___ has pierced my heart,___ So
fes - sion. If I don't see___ her each___ day___ An

be the truth con - fessed, Since cu - pid stung me
ill - ness I con - jure, Then just one look in

with his dart I'm fool - ish like the rest.
her sweet face will sure af - fect a cure.

poco rit.

CHORUS.

A dim - pled chin,——— An up - turned nose,——— Two

mp - f

cheeks that put——— to shame the rose,——— A daint - y mix - ture

made I am sure, To drive me mad, to tempt and al - lure. Two

JENNIE LEE.

Words by ARTHUR J. LAMB.

Music by HARRY VON TILZER.

I have come to take you home, Jen - nie
We will seek that shad - y dell, Jen - nie

Lee, To the heart that's al - ways yours, Jen - nie
Lee, Where our love we used to tell, Jen - nie

Lee, _____ Tho' your life is one re - gret, I am
Lee, _____ By the qui - et lit - tle stream, Where of

me true love you'll find, Jen - nie Lee ___
one who loves you best, Jen - nie Lee ___

CHORUS.

Jen - nie Lee, Sweet Jen - nie Lee, ___ No

fault with you I find, True love, sweet - heart is blind, Jen - nie

Lee, Tho' false to me, ___ You're my

lit - tle sweet - heart still, sweet Jen - nie Lee. ___

TELLER, SONS & DORNER. NEW-YORK.

Musical Supplement to the SUNDAY CHRONICLE

Chicago, Sunday, Mar. 31st 1901.

VIOLET

BY RAYMON MOORE

VIOLET.

Words & Music by Raymon Moore.

1. It was down by a brook, In a green, sha-dy nook, Oh, that morn I can
2. While we wan-der'd a-long, All the birds, in their song, Caroll'd sweet Till the

nev - er for-get! And I gave you a flow'r That I
bright sun had set, Then the stars up a-bove Seem'd to

pluck'd from a bow'r, A mod-est and sweet vi-o-let. Then I
beam with the love Of my sweetheart, my own vi-o-let. Now the

gazed in your eyes—They were blue as the skies—Near the wa-ters where
Sum-mer has fled, And the ros-es are dead, A fair lit-tle

riten. *a tempo*

rip-pling brooks met,_____ And I said you would be, Ev-er
flow'r lin-gers yet;_____ And it nev-er will fade, In the

riten. *a tempo*

af-ter, 'to me, My bright star, my own Vi-o-let._____
sun-light or shade.—'Tis the name you bear, sweet Vi-o-let._____

rit.

CHORUS

Oh, Vi - o - let,_____ don't for-get,_____ Vi - o -

p

Trust Me With Your Heart Again

TRUST ME WITH YOUR HEART AGAIN.

Words by Arthur Trevelyan.

Music by Gladys Millbrook.

1. I think some-times, my dear-est heart, Your love for me is grow-ing cold. And, you from me de-sire to part, Al-though you would the truth with-

2. Why tor-ture me with wild sus-pense? I'd noth-ing be if not your slave; Say what has been my true of-fence? And I'll a-tone for aught I

-hold;
gave.

You seem to doubt my love for you, I
Sweet-heart, why fear to trust in me, When

can - not help but won - der why, For should you ask if
all your woes I'd glad - ly bear? O speak, dear one, and

I am true, Ah! this is how I would re - ply:
so set free My throb - bing heart of all des - pair.

rall.

Moderato.

Not for Heav - en would I leave you Not for fortunes would I

grieve you, Not for a - ny - thing de - ceive you,

Do not sev - er Love's sweet chain; .... Life with you means naught but

glad - ness, Life with - out you naught but sad - ness;

rit. *rall.*

Yes, I love you e'en to mad - ness, Trust me with your heart a - gain.

rit. *rall.*

"I've a Longing in My Heart for You, Louise."

BY Chas. K. Harris.

Sung by ELLENE JAQUA.

AUTHOR OF
"AFTER THE BALL."
"BREAK THE NEWS TO MOTHER."
"MID THE GREENFIELDS OF VIRGINIA."
"FOR OLD TIMES SAKE."
AND OTHER FAMOUS HITS.

PUBLISHED BY
CHAS·K·HARRIS
MILW'AUKEE
AUTHOR OF THE WORLD FAMOUS SONG
"AFTER THE BALL"
NEW YORK   CHICAGO   LONDON

5

"I'VE A LONGING IN MY HEART FOR YOU, LOUISE."

BY THE AUTHOR OF THE WORLD-FAMOUS SONG AFTER THE BALL.

Arranged by JOS. CLAUDER.
Andante Espressivo.

Words and Music by CHAS. K. HARRIS.

1. I've a long-ing in my heart for you, Lou-ise, And I
2. Birds are sing-ing 'round the dear old south-ern home, And a

won-der if you al-so think of me, For your
dark-haired maid-en sits be-neath a tree, Think-ing

FREDERICK POLLWORTH & BRO., MUSIC TYPOGRAPHERS, MILWAUKEE.

sweet face haunts me ev - er, dear Lou - ise, And in
of her true love, ma - ny miles a - way, And she's

dreams I kiss your sweet lips ten - der - ly, I
won - d'ring if he'll ev - er con - stant be, When

seem to hear the old church chimes As in the by-gone days; I
soft up - on the sum - mer breeze She hears her name, Lou - ise: It

seem to hear the whipp-o'-wil's sad lay, And it

thrills her heart that beats for him a-lone, Then he

brings me back to you, my dear Lou-ise, And the

takes her in his arms so eag-er-ly, And he

gen-tle wav-ing corn-fields far a-way.

says: "I've come to claim you as my own."

CHORUS.

I've a long-ing in my heart for you, Lou - ise, And for the dear old sun - ny south - ern home, I can scent the hon - ey suck - le and the fra-grant jess - a - mine, I've a long-ing in my heart for you.

POPULAR SONG AND CHORUS.

WRITTEN & COMPOSED BY,

MR. MICHAEL. NOLAN.

LITTLE ANNIE ROONEY.

SUNG BY ALICE MAYDUE.

PUBLISHED BY HARDING BROS'

FOR SALE AT ALL MUSIC STORES PRICE 40.

Harding's Music Store. 229 Bowery. N. Y.

LITTLE ANNIE ROONEY.

Written, Composed, and Sung by MICHAEL NOLAN.

Arranged by GEORGE LE BRUN.

Tempo di Valce.

PIANO.

1. A win-ning way, a pleas-ant smile, Dress'd so neat but quite in style, Mer-ry chaff your time to wile, Has lit-tle An-nie Roon-ey.
2. The par-lor's small, but neat and clean, And set with taste so seldom seen, And you can bet, the household queen, Is lit-tle An-nie Roon-ey.
3. We've been en-gaged close on a year, The hap-py time is drawing near, I'll wed the one I love so dear, Lit-tle An-nie Roon-ey.

Published by HARDING BROS., 229 Bowery, New York.

Ev - ry ev' - ning, rain or shine, I make a call twixt eight and nine, On
The fire burns cheer - fully and bright, As a fami - ly cir - cle round each night, We
My friends de - clare I'm in a jest, Un - til the time comes will not rest, But

her who short - ly will be mine, Lit - tle An - nie Roon - - ey.
form and ev - ery one's de - light, Is lit - tle An - nie Roon - - ey.
one who knows its val - ue best, Is lit - tle An - nie Roon - - ey.

Chorus.
p, 2nd time ff.

She's my sweet - heart, I'm her beau; .... She's

my An - nie, ... I'm her Joe, ... Soon we'll

marry,..... nev-er..... to part,..... lit-tle An-nie

Roon-ey..... is my Sweet--heart!..... heart!.....

1 **2**

Dance.
Dolce.

Symphony.

Wm. H. Keyser & Co., Music Typographers, 921 Arch St., Phila.

WHEN THE·DAISIES·BLOOM

SONG BY

ANITA·OWEN

When The Daisies Bloom

Waltz Song

Words and Music by
ANITA OWEN

Tempo di Valse

Love, come with me —
I'll ne'er for - get —

O - ver the lea, Down where the .dai - sies grow. ——
When first we met, Here where the dai - sies grow. ——

You know full well   What I've to tell,   E - ven the dai - sies
Soft - ly I told   Love's sto - ry   old,   You mur-mured sweet and

know._____   Tho' we must part,   My faith - ful heart
low,_____   "Yes I will be   Faith - ful to thee,

With you shall e'er re - main,_____   For you I'll yearn Un -
My love is yours to claim,_____   Here is a kiss I

til my re - turn,   When dai - sies bloom a - gain._____
nev - er shall miss   Till dai - sies bloom a - gain."_____

LEONORA

THE MILLERS DAUGHTER

BY
BODINE & MAYWOOD.
Co AUTHORS OF

DORIS.
AMBOLENA SNOW.
FLY, YOU BLACKBIRDS, FLY.

SONG, 50.   WALTZ, 50.

Guitar. (Inst.). 40.   Two Mandolins and Guitar, 50.

Mandolin and Piano, 40.   Two Mandolins and Piano, 50.

Orchestra, 50.

GEO. SCHLEIFFARTH
(MAYWOOD)

Published by

THE S. BRAINARD'S SONS CO.
CHICAGO.

Copyright MDCCCXCVII by The S. Brainard's Sons Co

CHAS. SHEARD & CO., 192 High Holborn, London.

LEONORA

THE MILLER'S DAUGHTER.

Words by
LESTER BODINE.

Music by
GEO. MAYWOOD (Schleiffarth.)
Author of "Doris" etc., etc.

Introduction. *Moderato*

Tempo di Valse.

Con anima.

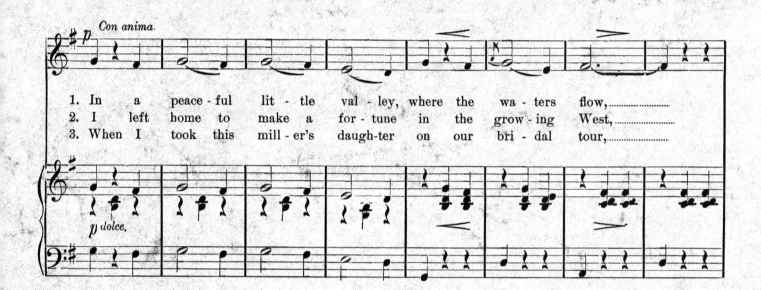

1. In a peace-ful lit-tle val-ley, where the wa-ters flow,............
2. I left home to make a for-tune in the grow-ing West,............
3. When I took this mill-er's daugh-ter on our bri-dal tour,............

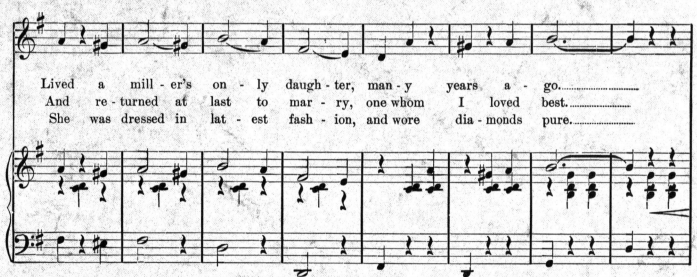

Lived a mill-er's on-ly daugh-ter, man-y years a-go............
And re-turned at last to mar-ry, one whom I loved best............
She was dressed in lat-est fash-ion, and wore dia-monds pure............

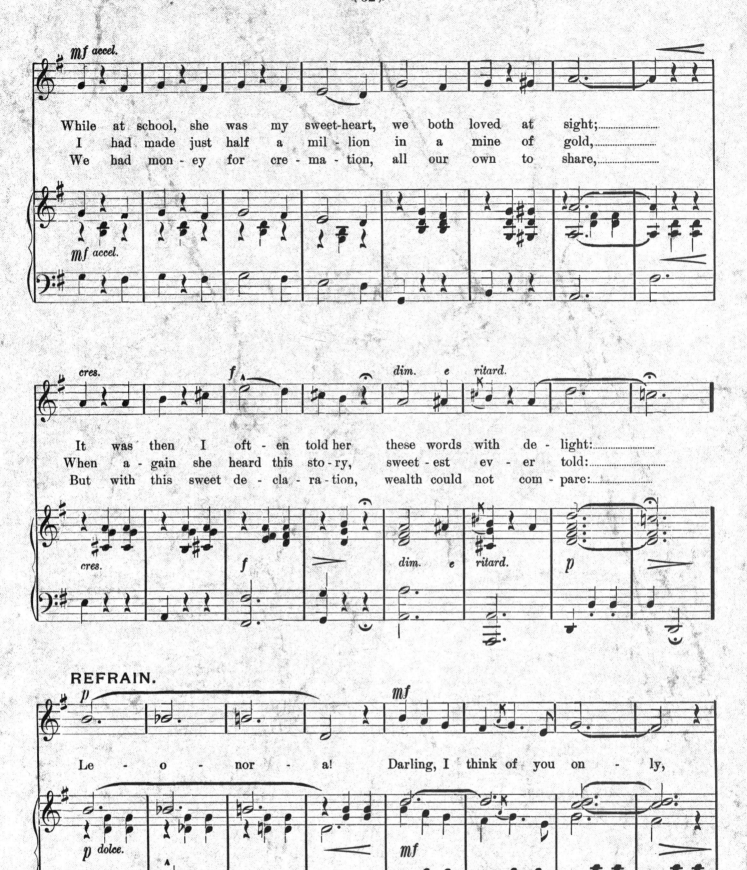

While at school, she was my sweet-heart, we both loved at sight;
I had made just half a mil-lion in a mine of gold,
We had mon-ey for cre-ma-tion, all our own to share,

It was then I oft-en told her these words with de-light:
When a-gain she heard this sto-ry, sweet-est ev-er told:
But with this sweet de-cla-ra-tion, wealth could not com-pare:

REFRAIN.

Le - o - nor - a! Darling, I think of you on - ly,

Le - o - nor - a! Life without you would be lone - ly.

Be mine, dear - est, And to my heart ev - er near - est,

Le - o - nor - a! Love me as I love you!.................... you!....................

MEREDITH, MUSIC PRINTER.

SHE WAS BRED IN OLD KENTUCKY.

Words by HARRY BRAISTED.

Music by STANLEY CARTER.

Moderato.

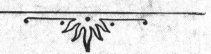

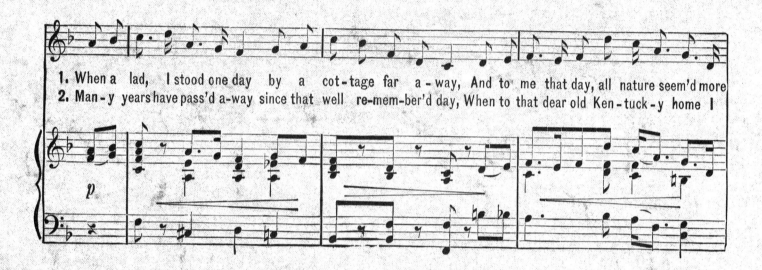

1. When a lad, I stood one day by a cot-tage far a-way, And to me that day, all nature seem'd more
2. Man-y years have pass'd a-way since that well re-mem-ber'd day, When to that dear old Ken-tuck-y home I

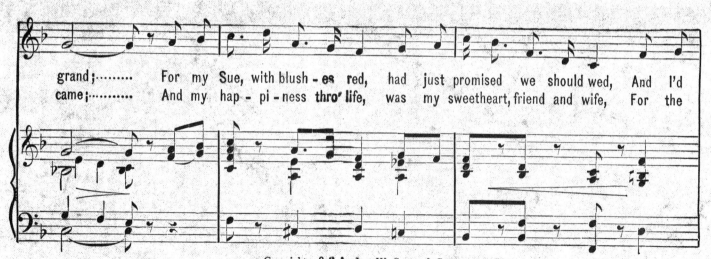

grand;.......... For my Sue, with blush-es red, had just promised we should wed, And I'd
came;.......... And my hap-pi-ness thro' life, was my sweetheart, friend and wife, For the

CHORUS.

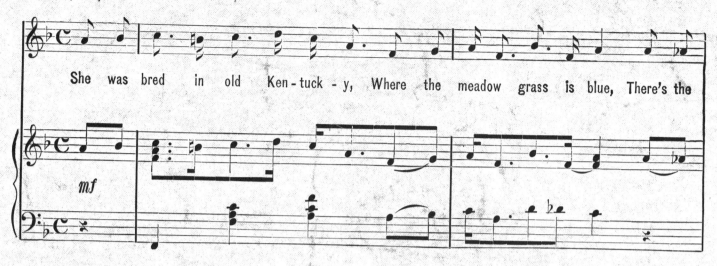

She was bred in old Ken-tuck-y, Where the meadow grass is blue, There's the

sun-shine of the country, in her face and man-ner too: She was bred in old Kentucky, Take her,

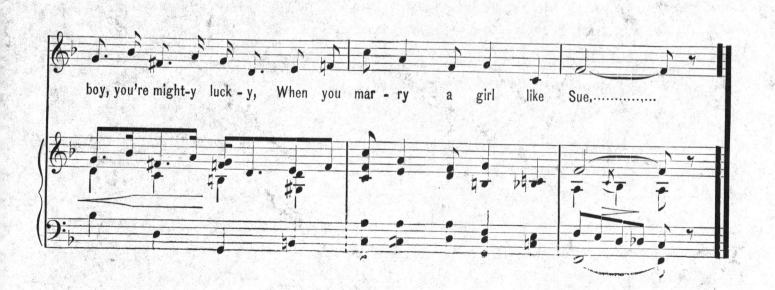

boy, you're might-y luck-y, When you mar-ry a girl like Sue,............,...

Introduced with great success by Helen May Butler and her Ladies' Military Band

WHERE THE SILV'RY COLORADO WENDS ITS WAY

THE ROYAL GORGE
ON THE LINE OF THE
DENVER & RIO GRANDE

WORDS BY
C. H. Scoggins

MUSIC BY
Chas. Avril

PUBLISHED BY
The Tolbert R. Ingram Music Co., Denver, Colo.
Chas. Sheard & Co., London, W.C.
COPYRIGHT, 1901, BY C. H. SCOGGINS AND CHAS. AVRIL.

Featured by REESE V. PROSSER in Al. G. Field's Minstrels

WHERE THE SILVERY COLORADO WENDS ITS WAY.

Words by C. H. SCOGGINS.

Music by CHARLES AVRIL.

Moderato.

The twi - light soft - ly gath - ers 'round my home a - mong the hills, And all
The sil - v'ry snow is gleam - ing on yon dis - tant moun-tain side, Where we

na - ture soon will set - tle down to rest, While I
oft - en used to wan - der, Nell and I, And the

sit and sad - ly pon - der and my heart with long - ing fills, As I
birds are gai - ly sing - ing in the val - ley far be - low, Where I

sil - v'ry Col - o - ra - do wends its way.
sil - v'ry Col - o - ra - do wends its way.

REFRAIN.

There's a sob on ev - 'ry breeze, And a sigh comes from the trees, And the

A tempo.

mead - ow - lark now croons a sad - der lay, For the sun-light plays no more 'round my

Rit.

cheer-less cab - in door, Where the sil - v'ry Col - o - ra - do wends its way.

"The Abyssinian Patrol," by Houseley, is a showy concert number

Sam F. Goss.
THE SEASON'S TREMENDOUS SUCCESS.
"SWEET ROSIE O'GRADY."
WALTZ SONG AND CHORUS.
Yours Truly Maude Nugent.
WRITTEN & COMPOSED BY
MAUDE NUGENT.
5
Published by JOS. W. STERN & Co 45 East 20th St New York.
LONDON, JOS. W. STERN & CO
Sole Agents, FRANK DEAN & CO., 31 Castle St., Oxford St., W., London.

SWEET ROSIE O'GRADY.

Words and Music by Maude Nugent.

Just down a-round the cor-ner of the street where I re-side, There
I nev-er shall for get the day she prom-ised to be mine, As

lives the cu-test lit-tle girl that I have ev-er spied; Her
we sat tell-ing love-tales, in the gold-en sum-mer time. 'Twas

name is Rose O' Gra-dy and, I don't mind tell-ing you, That
on her fin-ger that I placed a small en-gage-ment ring, While

she's the sweet-est lit-tle Rose the gar-den ev-er grew.
in the trees, the lit-tle birds this song they seemed to sing!

CHORUS. Valse.

Sweet Ro-sie O' Gra-dy, My dear lit-tle

Rose, She's my stea-dy la dy,

Most ev'-ry-one knows, And when we are mar - ried, How hap-py we'll be; I love sweet Ro - sie O' Gra - dy, And Ro - sie O' Gra - dy, loves me.

1.

2.

me

D.C

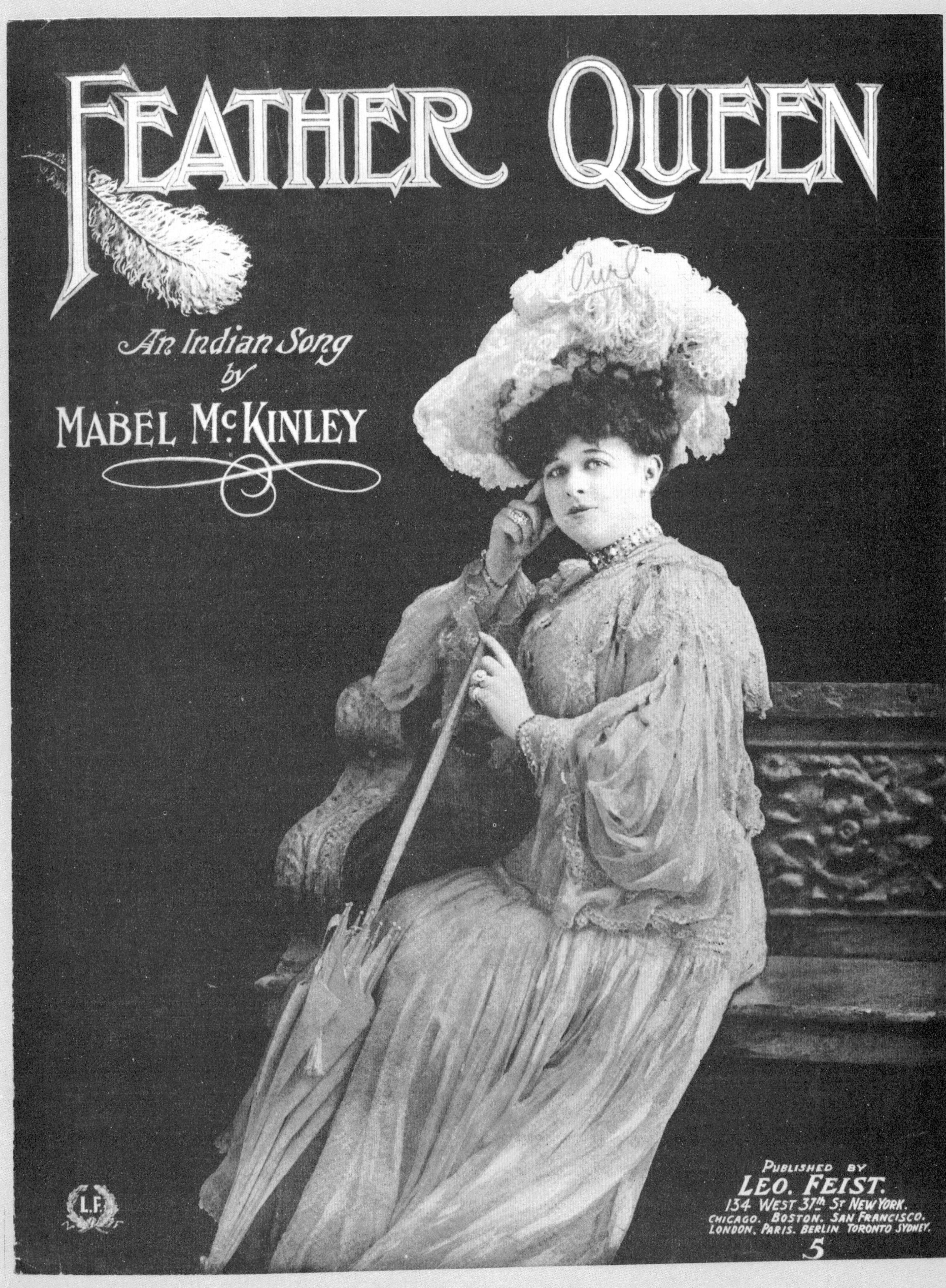

FEATHER QUEEN

An Indian Song
by
MABEL McKINLEY

PUBLISHED BY
LEO. FEIST.
134 WEST 37th ST. NEW YORK.
CHICAGO. BOSTON. SAN FRANCISCO.
LONDON. PARIS. BERLIN. TORONTO. SYDNEY.

5

Feather Queen.

Also published as an Intermezzo March-Two-Step.

MABEL M^C KINLEY.
Composer of "Anona," "Karama," etc.

Moderato.

Once an In-dian loved a chief-tain's daugh-ter,
Then the In-dian caught his fleet-est po - ny,

Sweet six-teen,___ quite se-rene,___ an In-dian Queen;___
Rode a-way,___ with-out de-lay,___ to town that day;___

Though she liked the brave who came to court her, Feather Queen,___ was a
Bought some clothes that made him look real "to - ny," Then re-turned,___ to his

sad co-quette, like girls I've seen! _____ She said "It's true, you've
Feather Queen, for whose love he yearned. _____ But, what a shame, for

come to woo, and I love you! ___ But still, you see, the man for me, a
when he came, she took the blame, _ And in distress, cried "change that dress, for

swell must be; _____ 'Tis the pale face ways I love!" Then he vowed by stars a-
I con-fess, _ You can't make a pale face man, Of a true-born In-di-

bove, That none but he should win this pret-ty Feather Queen! _____
an! You've won my heart, I'll be your lit-tle Feather Queen! _____

CHORUS.

When day is end - ed, And sun - set splen - did,

Bathes all the prai - rie, In gold and green! ___ Then I'll come

to you, ___ To fond-ly woo you, ___ Dear prai - rie fair - y, ___

___ My Feath - er Queen! ___ When day is Queen! ___

PRETTY KITTY DOYLE.

Words and Music by Roger Harding.

Moderato.

1. If ev-er you met her, You'd nev-er for-get her, My
2. Now, real-ly, I pi-ty The boys of this ci-ty For

pret-ty Kit-ty Doyle;......... The neigh-bors re-spect her, And
lov-ing Kit-ty Doyle;......... She cares for but one, He is

al-ways e-lect her To lead at a par-ty or ball.......... The
My fa-ther's son,—To the al-tar I'll lead Kit-ty Doyle.......... I'll

ANONA
VOCAL

By VIVIAN GREY
(Miss Mabel McKinley)

60

Published by *Leo Feist*, 134 West 37th Street. New York.
"Feist Building"
59 Dearborn St. Chicago, Ill.

ANONA.
(SONG.)

This Famous Composition is also published as an Intermezzo – Two Step – for Piano Price **60** cents, also for Band, Orchestra, Mandolin, Guitar, Banjo, Zither etc.

Moderato.

VIVIAN GREY.
(Miss Mabel McKinley.)

1. In the west-ern state of Ar-i-zo-na, Lived an Ind-ian maid;
2. When her fa-ther heard that his A-no-na, Loved this youth-ful brave;

She was called the beau-ti-ful A-no-na so 'tis said.
Straight-a-way he said he would dis-own her, things looked grave.

Grace-ful as a fawn was she, Just as sweet as she could be,
She must mar-ry "heap big chief," Sweet A-no-na hid her grief,

Eyes so bright, dark as night, Had this pret-ty lit-tle Ar-i-zo-na
Ran a-way, so they say, And got mar-ried to the man she loved with-

Ind-ian maid-en. All the chiefs who knew her, Came to woo her— For her pined
out de-lay-ing. Then her fa-ther sought her, Nev-er caught her, Till one day,

To mar-ry she de-clined, At last she changed her mind, But 'twas
When two years passed a-way, They both came back to stay, Then the

not a chief so grand, who won her heart and hand, But a
chief de-clared a truce, when they named their young pa-poose, Af-ter

war - rior bold, who wooed her with a song:_____
him and to his grand-child he would sing:_____ My sweet A-

Refrain.

no - na,___ in Ar-i - zo - na,___ There is no oth - er maid I'd

ser - e - nade;___ By camp-fires gleam-ing,___ of you I'm dream-ing,___ A - no-na,

my sweet Ind - ian maid._____ My sweet A- maid._____

FELLER, SONS & DORNER. NEW-YORK.

Musical Supplement to the SUNDAY CHRONICLE
Chicago, Sunday, Mar. 17th 1901.

GATH'RING THE SHAMROCKS WITH PATSIE

Dedicated by the AUTHOR
to
CALLIE MULVANEY

Words and Music
by
HARRY P. KEILY.

GATH'RING THE SHAMROCKS WITH PATSIE.

Words & Music by HARRY P. KEILY.

Tempo di Valse

1 There is a lit—tle sun—ny isle, Three thou—sand miles from
2 I think of hap—py twi—light hours, When in our home we'd

here,_____ And since I left its sham—rock shores, My life's been sad and
sit;_____ My dear old mo—ther, by the fire, Our stock—ings there would

drear._____ My heart mourns for the lov—ing ones, The friends so true and
knit;_____ My fa——ther would tell ma—ny tales Of Ire—land's wrongs and

kind._____ Each night and day I ev-er pray For those we left be-
woes._____ Then fai-ry sto-ries of our land, To us he would dis-

hind._____ I think of my dear pa-rents And my lit-tle sis-ter
close._____ The neigh-bors liv-ing 'round our place, Would make a friend-ly

too,_____ A-bro-ther fond and faith-ful, yes, Like him there are so
call;_____ The plea-sant song, the mer-ry dance Would be en-joyed by

few._____ How I wish that I could wan-der_____ In those fra-grant meadows
all._____ Then I'd steal a-way, so soft-ly,_____ In--to the meadows

green,_____ And greet my love, who vowed I was His dar-ling I-rish Queen.
green,_____ And greet my love, who vowed I was His dar-ling I-rish Queen.

CHORUS.

Then I'd go gath'-ring the shamrocks with Pat-sie,............ My blue-eyed I - rish

boy;............... Gath'ring the shamrocks with Pat-sie,........... He is my earth-ly

joy!........... I love my bonnie I - rish lad! My heart was full of glee,...............

rit.

Gath'-ring shamrocks with Pat-sie, Ah He's all the world to me!...............

rall.

GOOD-BYE, GOOD LUCK, GOD BLESS YOU

BALLAD

WORDS BY
J. KEIRN BRENNAN
MUSIC BY

ERNEST R. BALL

WRITERS OF
"A LITTLE BIT OF HEAVEN"
"IRELAND IS IRELAND TO ME"
"IN THE GARDEN OF THE GODS"
"IF IT TAKES A THOUSAND YEARS"
ETC. ETC.

M. WITMARK & SONS
NEW YORK   CHICAGO   LONDON

Good-bye, Good Luck, God Bless You

Is All That I Can Say

Words by
J. KEIRN BRENNAN

Music by
ERNEST R. BALL

It's hard to part when heart to heart We've lived and loved and dreamed.____ It
Though all that's bright and good and right To-day goes out with you,____ I'll
To arms, to arms! cry war's a-larms To call our boys a-way,____ Each

came to naught, al-though I thought That you were all you seemed.____ Though
al-ways pray there'll come a day When hope will live a-new:____ When
sol-dier lad in kha-ki clad Is ea-ger for the fray.____ And

I for-give, I can't for-get, I'll live with-in the past;____ That
love and trust from out the dust Of shat-tered dreams may rise;____ That
in that line, a pal of mine Is stand-ing big an strong;____ How

we have met I don't re-gret, I'll love you till the last.___
love now blind, may la-ter find A great-er Par-a-dise.___
I will yearn for his re-turn, I hope it won't be long.___

REFRAIN *Tenderly*

Good-bye, good luck, God bless you, Is all that I can say;___ But
Good-bye, good luck, God bless you, You're off to Mex-i-co,___ Tho'

when you leave, my heart will grieve For-ev-er and a day.___ Though oth-er
my heart's sad for you, my lad, I'm proud to see you go.___ Where du-ty's

arms ca-ress you, I can-not bid you stay;___ Good-bye, good
voice is call-ing, You brave-ly march a-way;___ Good-bye, good

luck, God bless you, Is all that I can say. Good-say.___
luck, God bless you, Is all that I can say. Good-say.___

My Farewell Don't Mean Good Bye.

Words by
AARON FEIST

Music by
HERBERT WALTERS
Arranged by
JOE NATHAN.

Marcia Moderato

Fare - well sweetheart mine, I must go,........................ My
My pic - ture then take ere we part,........................ For

heart aches to leave you be - hind;............... My boat's in the har - bor you
I have a good one of you;............... And dar - ling, it's fram'd in my

PART TWO

PATHETIC BALLADS

I'LL MARRY THE MAN·I·LOVE.

Sam F. Goss

BY THE COMPOSER OF MANY OF THE MOST BEAUTIFUL SONGS WRITTEN DURING THE PRESENT CENTURY SUCH AS "ALL HER FAULTS I LOVE HER STILL" "TAKE BACK YOUR GOLD" "MAKE ME YOUR WIFE" "FOR THE SAKE OF OUR DAUGHTER" ETC. ETC.

FROM A Melodious Standpoint THE MOST ORIGINAL SONG OF ITS KIND WRITTEN IN A DECADE

"GO! AND LET ME SEE YOUR FACE NO MORE!"

COPYRIGHT 1897

5

BY MONROE H. ROSENFELD AUTHOR OF "TAKE BACK YOUR GOLD" "IF YOU LOVE ME, LEAVE ME"

Published by JOS. W. STERN & CO. 45 East 20th St. New York

LONDON. JOS. W. STERN & CO. Sole Agents FRANK DEAN & CO. 31 Castle St. Oxford St. W. LONDON.
Copyright 1897 by Jos. W. Stern & Co. English Copyright and performing rights secured and reserved.

I'LL MARRY THE MAN I LOVE.

By MONROE H. ROSENFELD,

Composer of { "Take Back Your Gold;" "Just For the Sake of Our Daughter;" and other beautiful songs.

Moderato.

One day a rich man called his pretty daughter to his side, And
In an-ger proud he stormed and raged, then pointing to the door, Said:

said; "A wealthy friend of mine wants you to be his bride; Last
"Go! I cast you off, and let me see your face no more! You've

night he spoke to me and I have promised him your hand, So
dared to dis - o - bey me but your fol - ly you'll re - pent! For

when he calls, say you'll be his — re - - member my command!" The
out of all my millions you shall never have a cent!" She

maiden said,"Why fath - er, dear, I can - not be his wife, Be -
sad - ly turned to go but stopped be - side the door to say: " 'Tis

cresc. _

-cause I love an-oth-er, yes, far dear-er than my life!" And
you, not I, who will regret your cru-el words this day!" And

cresc. _ _ _ _ _ _ _ _ _ _ _ _ _ _ _ _ _ _ _

when he stern-ly told her she must wed his choice, in-stead, Or
when he said, "Well, I'll-for give if you will on-ly wed The

rit.   *a tem.*

else he'd dis-in-her-it her, she wept but staunchly said:
man I've chosen for you, dear," once more she bravely said:

rit.   *a tem.*

f

Tempo di Valse.

"I'll marry the man I love .... No other my hand shall claim .... For I've

given my heart to him, dad, And some day I'll bear his name .... Re-

member that gold can't buy .... Or conquer a woman's heart .... And I'll

marry the man I love, dad, Tho' from you I part!" ....

A Story in Song of Hearts & Flowers.

ONLY A BUNCH OF VIOLETS

WORDS BY
ANDREW B. STERLING

MUSIC BY
C·M·VANDERSLOOT

5

Song   50.
Piano Solo (way) 50.
Male Quartette   25.
Orchestra   75

Also Published for
Mandolin
Guitar & Piano.

VANDERSLOOT
MUSIC Co.,
Williamsport
Penn'a

Only a Bunch of Violets.

Words by ANDREW B. STERLING.

Music by C. M. VANDERSLOOT.
Arr. by LEE OREAN SMITH.

Andante moderato.

1. The gay ball-room was crowd-ed, the lights were shin-ing bright, A
2. The cold gray dawn was creep-ing, the strains of "Home, Sweet, Home," Were

maid-en and a lad stood side by side,___ He said, "Al-though we've quarreled, I
soft-ly played so sim-ple yet so grand,___ The ball-room was in dark-ness, A

bring to you to-night, An of-fer-ing of peace," then soft-ly sighed;___ "'Tis
lad stood all a-lone, He held a bunch of vio-lets in his hand;___ He

just a bunch of vi - o - lets still wet with Heav - en's dew, I
gent - ly press'd them to his lips and soft - ly said "Good-bye," And

plucked them in the fields for you to - day,_____ She
then a pis - tol shot rang loud and clear,_____ And

took them from his hand and cried, "My love for you is dead," Then
with his life's tide ebb - ing fast, he whis-pered once a - gain; "You

cast the bunch of vi - o - lets a - way._____
did not know how much I loved you, dear."_____

poco rall.

CHORUS.

On - ly a bunch of— vi - o-lets With—ered and dy-ing a - lone,—

Cast by a maid on a ball-room floor, It spoke of a love that had flown;—

Trampled and crush'd by the danc-ing throng, How quick-ly a maid-en for - gets,— It

told it's sad tale of a brok - en heart, That bunch of sweet vi - o - lets.—

TELLER, SONS & DORNER. NEW-YORK.

Those Wedding Bells Shall Not Ring Out.

Illustrated & Sung by MAXWELL & SIMPSON

IMOGENE COMER

WILL S. SING

HELENE MORA

J. ALDRICH LIBBEY

JULIE MACKEY

Yours Truly Helene Mora

50

WORDS & MUSIC by MONROE H. ROSENFELD.

Published by CHAS. W. HELD, Brooklyn N.Y.

LONDON, W.C. ENGLAND, CHAS. SHEARD & CO.

Copyright MDCCCXCVI by CHAS. W. HELD   English Copyright Secured.

Those Wedding Bells Shall Not Ring Out!

Words and Music by MONROE H. ROSENFELD,
Author of
"THE SONG OF THE STEEPLE." "WITH ALL HER FAULTS
I LOVE HER STILL." AND MANY POPULAR WORKS.

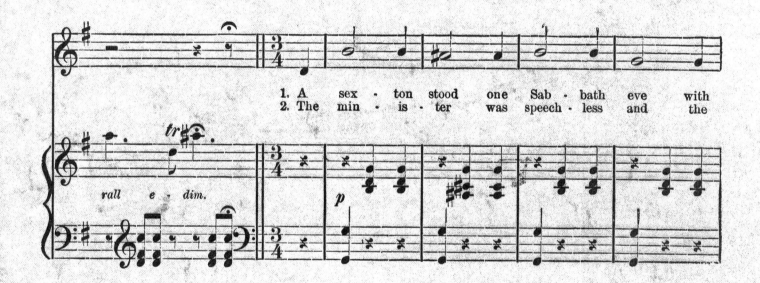

1. A sex - ton stood one Sab - bath eve with
2. The min - is - ter was speech - less and the

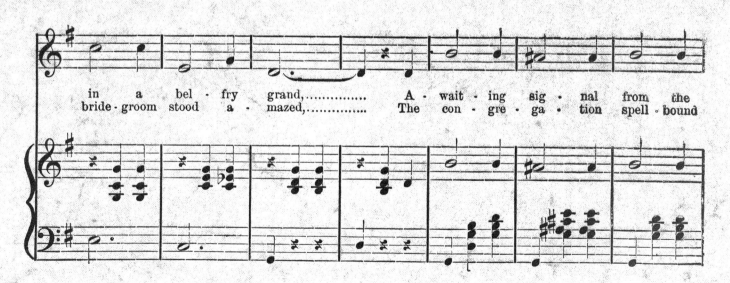

in a bel - fry grand,.............. A - wait - ing sig - nal from the
bride - groom stood a - mazed,.............. The con - gre - ga - tion spell - bound

church with bell - rope in his hand;.............. As in the house of
sat and thought the man was crazed,............ The bride had not a

wor - ship stood a young and hap - py pair.............. To pledge their
word to say, but sim - ply hung her head............ "Who is this

troth for - ev - er - more each oth - er's love to share.............. The
man?" the preacher asked, "I know him not," she said................ "Then

ho - ly man then spake these words: "Be - fore you're joined for life.................. Has
ring the bells," the bride - groom cried— the man knelt to en - treat—............ The

a - ny per - son aught to say 'gainst you, as man and
sex - ton swung the chimes a - loft, the bells rang clear and

wife!"............. Then, down the aisle there came a man with
sweet;............. But scarce their mu - sic had be - gun when

quick and ea - ger tread,............... And, point - ing to the
forth there came a shout:............... "Stand back! I say, they

tremb - ling bride, these words he calm - ly said:...............
shall not ring, those bells shall not ring out!"...............

Chorus.

After first and second verses ff.   After third verse pp.

1. "Those wed-ding bells must not ring out, She is an-oth-er's bride, I
2. "Those wed-ding bells shall not ring out, I swear it on my life! For
3. "Those wed-ding bells shall not ring out, I swear it on my life! For

saw her at the al-tar-rail, We stood there side by side; She can-not claim an-oth-er's hand—She
we were wed-ded years a-go And she is still my wife! She shall not break her vows to me—She's
we were wed-ded years a-go And she is still my wife! She shall not break her vows to me—She's

dare not break the law's command—A guilt-y wife you see her stand! Those bells shall not ring out."
mine through all e-ter-ni-ty—She's mine till death shall set her free—Those bells shall not ring out!"
mine through all e-ter-ni-ty—She's mine till death shall set her free—Those bells shall not ring out!"

D. C.

rall.

Molto agitato.

3. A shriek of woe—a glit-'ring blade—a lurch— a flash— a dart— And,

like the lightning's stroke, the blade had reach'd her trembling heart. "You've kill'd his bride—oh God!" they cried! He

piu lento.

swung the gleaming knife, And pierc'd his own heart as he gasp'd: "Nay, not his bride— *my wife!*" Two

The Beautiful Narrative Ballad

TAKE BACK YOUR GOLD

Sam F. Goss

SUNG WITH UNBOUNDED SUCCESS BY THE SWEET-VOICED BOY TENOR MASTER JOHN J. QUIGLEY FRED. SALCOMBE AND OTHER NOTED BALLADISTS

ALSO SUNG BY THE AUTHOR THE POPULAR TENOR IN PRIMROSE AND WEST'S MINSTRELS 3 ENCORES NIGHTLY

WORDS BY LOUIS W. PRITZKOW AUTHOR OF "HIS ONLY WISH" ETC.

MUSIC BY MONROE H. ROSENFELD COMPOSER OF "DON'T SEND HER AWAY" "WITH ALL HER FAULTS I LOVE HER STILL" ETC

AND MAKE ME YOUR WIFE

5

Published by JOS. W. STERN & CO 45 East 20th St New York.

LONDON, JOS. W. STERN & CO
Sole Agents, FRANK DEAN & CO. 31 Castle St. Oxford St., W. London.

TAKE BACK YOUR GOLD.

Written by Louis W. Pritzkow.

Composed by Monroe H. Rosenfeld.

Andante moderato.

saw a youth and maid-en on a lone-ly ci-ty street, And
drew her close un-to him and to soothe her then he tried, But

thought them lov - ers, at their meet - ing place;............................. Un -
she in pride and sor - row turned a - way, ... And

-til, as I drew near, I heard the girl's sad voice en - treat The
as he sought to com - fort her, she wept and soft - ly sighed, "You'll

one who heed - ed not her tear-stained face.............................. " I
rue your cru - el ac - tions, Jack, some day."............................. "Now,

on - ly ask you, Jack, to do your du - ty, that is all. You
lit - tle one, don't cry," he said "for though to-night we part, And

know you promised that we should be wed."............... And
though an - oth - er soon will be my bride,............... This

when he said, "You shall not want, what - ev - er may be - fall," She
gold will help you to for - get," but with a break ing heart, She

spurned the gold he of - fered her and said :...............
scorned his gift and bit - ter - ly re - plied :...............

CHORUS.

"Take back your gold, for gold can nev-er buy me; Take back your bribe, and

promise you'll be true; Give me the love, the love that you'd de-ny me;

Make me your wife, that's all I ask of you!"

rall. - e - dim.

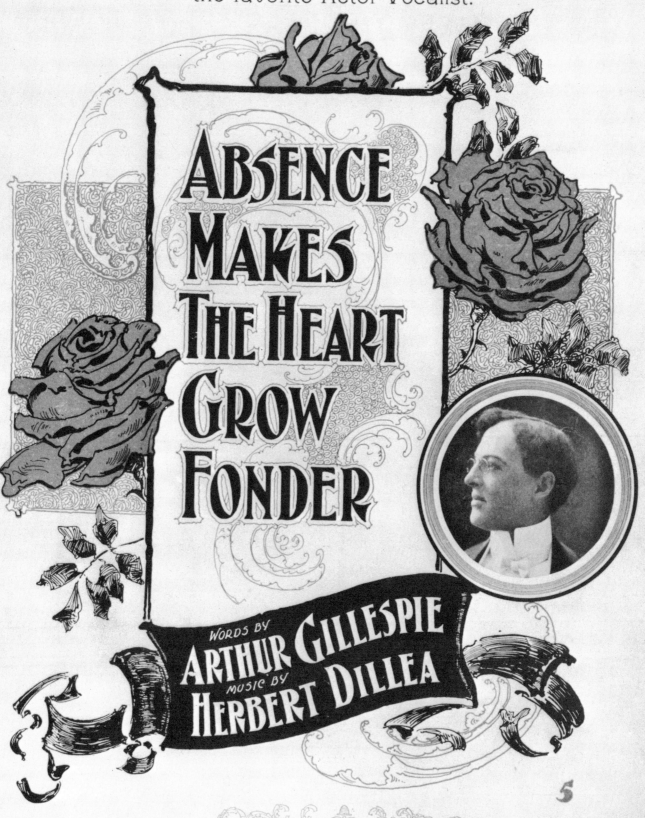

ABSENCE MAKES THE HEART GROW FONDER.

(LONGING TO BE NEAR YOUP SIDE.)

Words by ARTHUR GILLESPIE.　　　　　Music by HERBERT DILLEA.

Andante con moto.

1. Sweet-heart I have grown so lone-ly, Liv-ing thus a-way from you,
2. Has the love that once was dear-er Than all else to me grown cold?

For I love you and you on-ly; Still I won-der if you're true.
Or has ab-sence drawn us near-er, To each oth-er as of old?

I re-gret the harsh words spo-ken, That I know have caused you pain,
Prom-ise then you will not sev-er From the ties that bind us two.

And my heart is near-ly bro-ken, Say you love me once a-gain......
Say you will be mine for-ev-er, Tell me that you still are true......

CHORUS.

Ab-sence makes the heart grow fond - - er, That is why I long for you;....

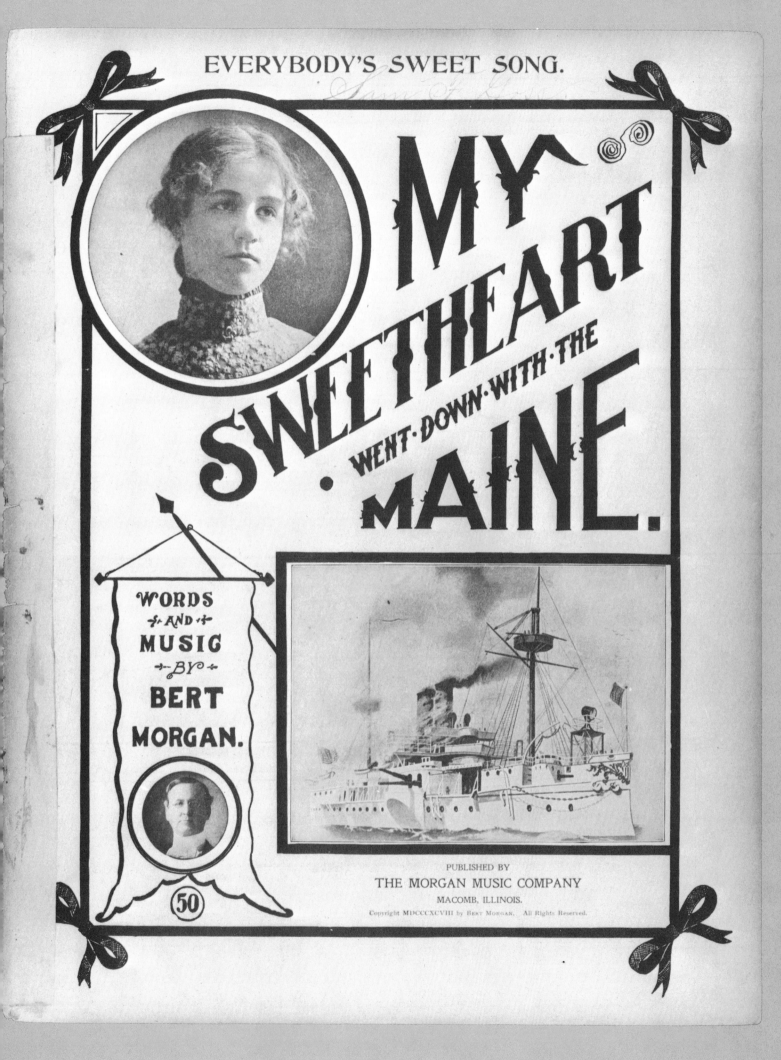

"'Tis better to have loved and lost,
Than never to have loved at all."

NOTE.—At 9:40 p. m., February 15, 1898, the United States Battle Ship Maine, anchored at Havana, Cuba, was "blown up" and sunk, carrying down 266 Officers, Sailors and Marines doing service in Uncle Sam's Navy. One of these unfortunates, who now lies buried in Havana in an unknown grave, was the betrothed of Miss Frances N——, of ——, Illinois, the 30th of May having been decided upon for the wedding day, and to her (and with her permission) I respectfully dedicate this song.—B. M.

My Sweetheart Went Down With The Maine.

Moderato.

Words and Music by BERT MORGAN.

1. Once I had a sweet-heart, no-ble, brave and true..........
2. Anchored at Ha-va--na on the Cu-ban shore..........
3. Buried in a foreign land, in an un-known grave..........

Fear-less as the sun-rise, gen-tle as the dew..........
Conscious of no dan-ger, dream-ing love days o'er;..........
Where the bells of liber-ty, soon must ring to save;..........

We had loved and wait - ed, he had named the day_____ And
Peace-ful - ly the slum - bered, in his ham - mock bed_____ And
Peace-ful - ly he slumbers still, 'neath a tor - rid sun_____ And

we had pledged to wed each oth - er, in the month of May,_____ And
While the stars with glow - ing beau - ty, ben - e - dic - tions said,_____ And
through all time, 'twill bleed for him, this heart, this heart he won,_____ And

we had pledged to wed each oth - er, in the month of May_____
While the stars with glow - ing beau - ty, ben - e - dic - tions said_____
through all time 'twill bleed for him, this heart, this heart he won_____

Out on   the high seas he   sailed,............................   un - der the "Red White and Blue,"............................
Then came a death dealing crash,............................ wrecking the ves - sel in   twain,............................
Rouse ye, my coun-try-men, rouse,............................ let not his death be in   vain,............................

Faith-ful   to coun-try and home,............................ Faith-ful   to cap-tain and   crew............................
Down went my sweet-heart to death,............................ Down went our gal-lant ship Maine............................
Strike down the cow-ard - ly fiends............................ Who slaughtered the crew of the   Maine............................

CHORUS.

1.–2. Once I   had   a   sweet - heart,   no-ble,   brave and   true............................
3.   Once I   had   a   sweet - heart,   no-ble,   brave and   true............................

Fear-less as the sun - rise, gen-tle as the dew............

We had loved and wait - ed, he had named the day,............ And

we had pledged to wed each oth - er, in the month of May............

rit. *tempo.*

Since DADDY'S been Taken Away.

POST OFFICE.

STAMPS

A Pathetic Ballad by HOWARD and EMERSON

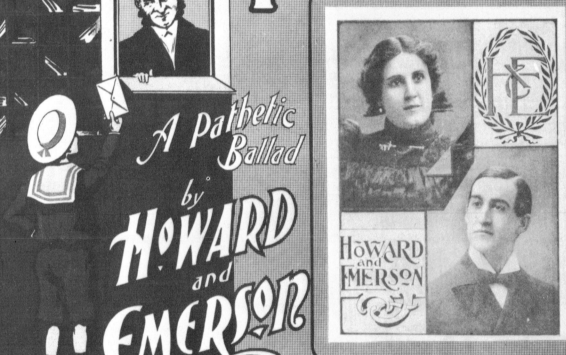

and Maurice J. Steinberg.

PUBLISHED BY SHAPIRO, BERNSTEIN & VON TILZER
NEW YORK 45 WEST 28th St
CHICAGO, 55 DEARBORN St

Since Daddy's Been Taken Away.

3

Words and Music by
HOWARD & EMERSON.
and
MAURICE J. STEINBERG.

1. The of-fice was bu-sy 'twas near close of
2. "Who sent you" the clerk asked in tones soft and

day and a good na-tured crowd stood in line,_____
low as he thought of two tots of his own,_____

Wait-ing to mail to their friends far a-way,
"Came by my-self" said the lad "Ma don't know, I

Copyright 1901 by Shapiro, Bernstein & Von Tilzer.
45 W. 28th St. New York. 53 Dearborn St. Chicago, Ill.

To_kens for gay Christ_mas time,_____ To the clerk at the
left her at home all a_lone,_____ Since dad_dy's been

win_dow a lit_tle lad ran and the crowd wait_ing there, stepped a_
tak_en our house don't seem bright and I nev_er see ma_ma dear

side._____ "What is yours" asked the clerk "now my bright lit_tle
smile._____ So I thought if I sent dad a let_ter to_

rall.

man", Then the tot in a sweet voice re_plied:_____
night, He would come back to us for a while."

CHORUS.
Espressivo

"Here's a let_ter to dad _ _ dy, He's in Heav_en you know, _____

Take good care of it, please do, For I want to be sure it will go, _____ If

dad _ dy writes back an ans _ wer send it with_out de _ lay, _____ For

ma_ma and I are so lone_ly now, since dad_dy's been tak_en a way."

rall. e dim.

TELLER, SONS & DORNER. NEW-YORK.

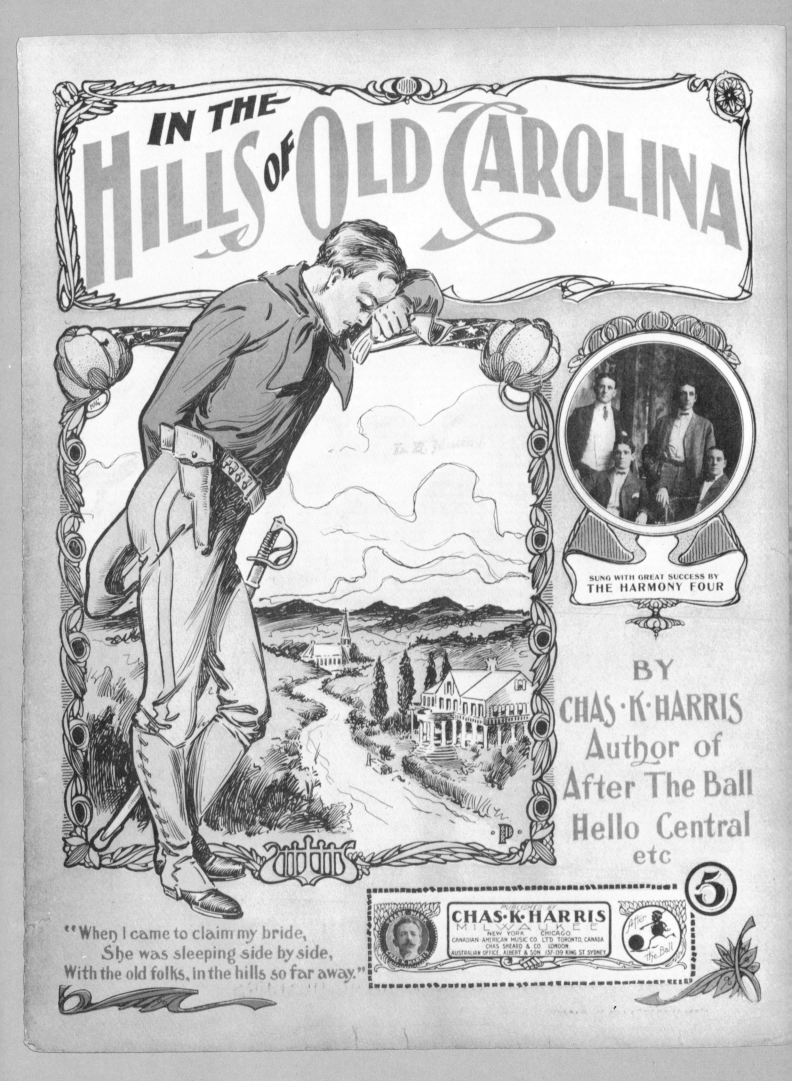

"In the Hills of Old Carolina."

BY THE AUTHOR OF THE WORLD-FAMOUS SONG AFTER THE BALL.

Words and Music by CHAS. K. HARRIS.

Arranged by JOS. CLAUDER.

1. In the hills of old Car - o - lina, Where the ro - ses ev - er bloom, And the
2. Ah, how well do I re - mem-ber, When we part - ed by the brook, Then the

hon - ey - suck - le breathes its rare per-fume,   Where all na-ture seems to play, While the
moon shone on her pale and sad - dened look,   When I said good-bye Elaine, I'll come

birds sing sweet their lay, 'Tis the home of one whom I do love so dear, And in
back to you a - gain, For with - out your love my life is naught but pain; Then the

fan - cy oft I see her Strol-ling through the vil - lage green, Hear her
cru - el war's com - mands Made the Blue and Gray join hands, We

laugh-ter rip - pling cheer - ful - ly and gay, Ah, how hap - py all did seem, When a-
fought like com - rades old in ev - 'ry fray; When I came to claim my bride, She was

lone we'd sit and dream, In the hills of old Car - o - lina far a - way.
sleep - ing side by side, With the old folks, in the hills so far a - way.

CHORUS.

In the hills of old Car - o - lina, Stands a dear old south - ern home, Where

oft' in child-hood days We used to play, Now the one I loved so well, Sleeps where

weep - ing wil - lows dwell, In the hills of old Car - o - lina, far a - way.

"YOUR MOTHER WANTS YOU HOME, BOY,
AND SHE WANTS YOU MIGHTY BAD."

SUNG WITH GREAT SUCCESS BY

R. J. JOSE

WRITTEN & COMPOSED BY

PAUL DRESSER.

3

Your Mother Wants You Home, Boy.
(And She Wants You Mighty Bad.)

By PAUL DRESSER.

A moth - er near a win - dow on a storm - y win - ter's night
Poor soul, she's growing wea - ry, wea - ry watch - ing day by day

Thinks of one who wandered from the fold, The tie that binds her heartstrings is
With the flame of hope still in her eye, Just like a good old mother, a

bro - ken and she prays In si - lence to the shep - herd king of
something in her heart Has whis - pered "He is com - ing bye and

old; For years she nev - er fal - tered knowing that the clouds would break The
bye." At last the pray'r is answered, don't you hear the rust - ling leaves A

lamp in her heart nev - er fails to burn, In some far dis - tant ci - ty a
step, she knows it, then a cry of joy Oh, moth - er I am with you, he

wan - d'rer hears a voice, The voice of moth - er bid - ding him re - turn.
takes her in his arms And all that she can say is "Tom my boy!"

When You were Sweet Sixteen.

SONG AND CHORUS.

Words and Music by JAMES THORNTON.

1. When first I saw the love-light in your eye,....... And heard thy voice, like sweet-est mel-o-
2. Last night I dreamt I held your hand in mine,....... And once a-gain you were my hap-py

dy,....... Speak words of love to my en-rap-tur'd soul,......... The
bride...... I kiss'd you as I did in Auld Lang Syne,........ As

world had naught but joy in store for me.......... E'en though we're drift-ing down life's stream a-
to the church we wan-der'd side by side......... The love I bear for you can nev - er

part,.......... Your face I still can see in dream's do - main;....... I
die;.......... With - out you, I had rath - er not been born;....... And,

know that it would ease my breaking heart........ To hold you in my arms just once a - gain.....
ev - en tho' we nev - er meet a - gain,........ I love you as the sun-shine loves the morn. ....

CHORUS.

Slower.

I love you 3 I nev - er lov'd be - fore,.......... Since

first I met you on the vil - lage green...... Come to me, or my dream of love is

o'er........ I love you as I lov'd you When you were sweet, when you were sweet sixteen.

Molto rall. *a tempo.*

LOOK FOR ME WHEN THE LILACS BLOOM!

Words and Music by

RICHARD H. GERARD

FRANK A. NANKIVELL 1906

LOOK FOR ME WHEN THE LILACS BLOOM

Words & Music by RICHARD H GERARD.
Author of "In the Golden Autumn time, sweet Elaine," "Good by Glory," "Sweet Adeline"

They came at twi-light as the sun in glo-ry Brought
Her lov-ing heart has sigh'd and long grown wea-ry, For

rest to bloom-ing na-ture's Spring-time day; By
some-one's fair face she still waits in vain; The

meadow brook he whisper'd love's old sto-ry, To her the fu-ture seem'd a pic-ture
li-lacs bloom'd but days to her seem'd dreary, He said at Springtime he'd re-turn a-

gay............... "We ne'er will part" he said, and she be-
gain............... But in a for-eign land to-night he's

liev - ing, Could nev - er doubt the words she heard him
sleep - ing, Wrapped in the flag he fought to keep on

say;............... His coun-try called, a - lone he left her
high;............... And when the twi - light shad - ows come a -

griev - ing, And murmured when he said good bye one day:...............
creep - ing, Her heart grown sad, his fond words seem to sigh:...............

CHORUS

Look for me when the li - lacs bloom, And the birds sing sweet in

Spring,........ When the air is filled with a sweet per - fume And the

bells at twilight ring..... I'll come back with a heart that's true, Tho' I

leave you now in gloom,........ When the cru-el war is thro' With a

heart that's fond and true, Look for me when the li - lacs bloom.........

The Wood Nymph

AS SUNG BY

Marguerita Sylva

IN THE
COMIC OPERA SUCCESS

THE PRINCESS CHIC

WORDS BY
KIRKE LA SHELLE

MUSIC BY
JULIAN EDWARDS

THE WOOD NYMPH AND THE RIVER GOD.

As sung by

"PRINCESS CHIC."

Words by KIRKE LA SHELLE.

Music by JULIAN EDWARDS.

Moderately slow.

1. A wood nymph lived
2. Her love to him

in an old oak tree On a riv-er's bank in a for-est fair
did she sweet-ly give, His passion for her was plain to see

And once on a time she chanced to see A riv-er god in the
But on-ly in wa-ter could he live And she in the heart of the

wa - ter there........... She thrill'd as she looked
old oak tree. .... So she pined and pined

.... on his no - -ble face, Her love she voiced.....
with ma - ny a sigh, And her heart ached so ....

.... in a joy - ous song; And he........ was en - rap-tured with her
.... with each pass - ing day That the oak,........ pity-ing her, did

grace, And wor - shipped her........... from the reeds a - mong........
die, — And thus the wood nymph passed a - way........

Slow and sustained.

Poor lit-tle nymph in her old oak tree, Poor riv-er god in the crystal wave,

pp

He would have joyed in the wood to be, And she in the wa-ter cool to lave.

Poor wood nymph and riv-er god too,

cresc.

What.......... could they do? What could they do?

D.C.

A True Song Story

An Hour Too Late!

VOL. III. NO. 296.

MOTHER KILLS SELF AND BOY

Pitiful Tragedy in a Rooming House on Oak Street.

SUFFOCATED BY GAS.

Kate ———, of ———, Mo., Opens the Door for Death.

She Tried Faithfully for Work, but Could Not Find It.

LETTER CAME TOO LATE.

DELAYED AN HOUR IN DELIVERY.

It Contained a Dollar Bill, and Its Prompt Delivery Might Have Averted the Tragedy.

Mrs. Kate ——— and her 3-year-old son George were discovered dead in their room at the lodging house 603 Oak St.

WORDS BY
HORACE HURON.
MUSIC BY
W. M. BARNES.

ALSO COMPOSER OF
"THE WREN" (POLKA CAPRICE)
"WOMAN'S WITCHERY WALTZES.
"JUNGLE THOUGHTS" (GAVOTTE)
"RAG PICKERS DANCE"—

5

AGAIN TOO LATE!

More Money That Would Have Saved Two Lives.

CAME BY MAIL TO-DAY.

Pathetic Feature Added to Yesterday's Sad Tragedy.

Kate ——— Fought Vainly, as She Thought, Against Fate.

HUSBAND HEARTBROKEN.

He Had Sent Her $3 in Addition to the $1 Sent Tuesday

PUBLISHED BY
HORACE HURON.

ROCK ISLAND, ILL.

AN HOUR TOO LATE.

Words by HORACE HURON.

Music by W. M. BARNES.

Andante Moderato.

In a lit‑tle at‑tic room   A‑mid pov‑er‑ty and gloom, They
Who can tell us of the strife   She had made to keep her life, As from

found a moth‑er and her lit‑tle child,   Ly‑ing
day to day she walked the bus‑y street,   While the

cold up_on the bed, From life's strug_gle she had fled, She had
land_lord said in scorn, "Pay your rent or else be_gone," Crazed with

sought for work but fail_ure drove her wild. Her fond
hun_ger found her mis_er_y com_plete. When a

hus_band far a_way, Work_ing hard from day to day, From the
wom_an, hon_est, pure, Tries to keep her soul se_cure, Would

vil_lage shop a let_ter he had sent; Wrote of
rath_er die than yield to Sa_tan's art; In de_

wag _ es grow _ ing less, From a heart in deep dis _ tress, "Here's a
spair with ach _ ing head, Hears her ba _ by cry for bread, Who can

dol _ lar it will help to pay your rent".
say 'twas crime? 'twas but a brok _ en heart.

rit.

Refrain.
Tempo di Valse

It was just an hour too late _____ They have passed thro' the

mf

gol _ den gate, _____ Tho' help is nigh their spir _ its

fly   To a   land where happiness waits,_____   Still

joyous the banquet and ball,_____ "Why   heed   dull

poverty's call?"_____   Fond   hearts   are   crushed   Loved

voices are hushed! For his letter   came   too   late._____

D. C. Intro.

Supplement to the SUNDAY CHRONICLE   Chicago, Sunday, Jan. 27th 1901.

Treasures that Gold cannot buy

WORDS AND MUSIC
BY
WILL A. HEELAN

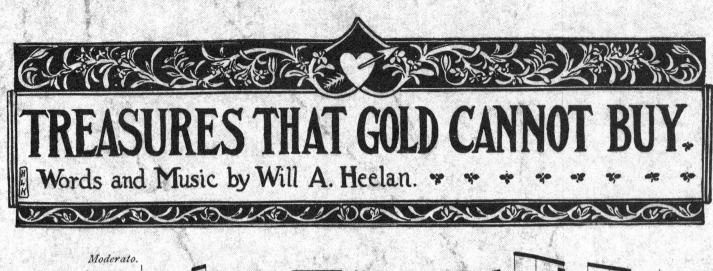

TREASURES THAT GOLD CANNOT BUY.

Words and Music by Will A. Heelan.

1. Sad are the mem-'ries, yet sweet in their sad-ness, I see in fan-cy my
2. Far from the old scenes I roam brok-en-heart-ed, Far from the sweet-heart I'll

old home once more, Gai-ly the birds sing their fresh song of glad-ness,
ne'er see a-gain. Un-der the wil-lows in si-lence we part-ed,

Iv - y - vines creep round the old cot - tage door. Deep in the wild - wood where
When she had told me my love was in vain. Fond - ly I gaze at her

shy vio - lets flow - er, There we would wan - der— my moth - er and I.
pic - ture, be - seech - ing Time to turn back - ward; then tears dim my eye.

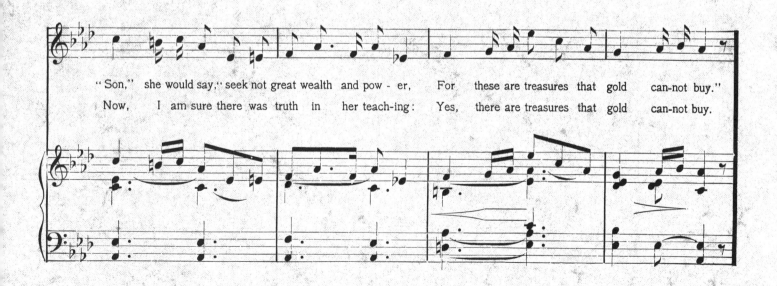

"Son," she would say, "seek not great wealth and pow - er, For these are treasures that gold can-not buy."
Now, I am sure there was truth in her teach-ing: Yes, there are treasures that gold can-not buy.

REFRAIN. *Espressivo.*

"The love that you long for; a sweet, ten - der tok - en, Though its

mem - o - ry brings but a tear or a sigh, A day gone for - ev - er; a

word left un - spok - en; All these are treas - ures that gold can - not buy."

Treasures That Gold Cannot Buy.   3 pp—3d p.

IN THE SHADE
OF THE
OLD APPLE TREE

WORDS
BY
HARRY
WILLIAMS

EMPIRE CITY QUARTETTE

MUSIC
BY
EGBERT
VAN ALSTYNE

In the Shade of the Old Apple Tree.

Words by
HARRY H. WILLIAMS.

Music by
EGBERT VAN ALSTYNE.

1. The o-ri-ole with joy was sweet-ly sing-ing,_____ The
2. I've real-ly come a long way from the cit-y,_____ Ard

lit-tle brook was bab'-ling it's tune,___ The vil-lage bells at noon were gai-ly
though my heart is break-ing I'll be brave,___ I've brought this bunch of flow'rs I think they're

ring-ing ____ The world seem'd bright-er than a har-vest moon;___ For
pret-ty ____ To place up-on a fresh-ly mould-ed grave;___ If

THEY ARE JUST THE SAME TO DAY

WORDS AND MUSIC BY

HORACE HURON

He also wrote
BRUSH THE FROWNS AWAY
THE VOLUNTEERS LAST GOOD BYE
De San Mans A Comin
and TOO LATE

Trade Supplied By
C.L. PARTEE MUSIC CO.
NEW YORK.

5

PUBLISHED BY
HORACE HURON,
ROCK ISLAND ILLS

They Are Just The Same To Day.

HORACE HURON.

Tempo di Valse.

VOICE.

1. Down the   street there came
2. But __   not far be -

pass - ing a migh - ty   throng   of the wealth   of a ci - ty
hind in an old creak - ing   cart   came an - oth - er un - not - iced a -

grand _____   There were strains of sweet mu - sic in   slow mar - tial
lone _____   The __ un - paint - ed box of the   pau - per we

time, 'twas the migh - ti - est one in the land,_____ From

saw, and we said "it is bet - ter he's gone."_____ There were

car - riag - es pass - ing the flash - ing of gems, and the glimmer of

on - ly two mourners they rode on the cart, a___ boy and a

silk and lace_____ A hearse filled with flowers and with

sweet lit - tle girl_____ Their clothes were in rags and their

deep sa - ble drapes, bore him home to his last resting place._____

lit - tle feet bare two poor orph - ans cast out on the world._____

CHORUS.

They are just the same to-day They are go-ing the same old way ____ Their sto-ry is told now in six feet of mold, And is fin-ished for - ev - er and aye ____ Of their pride we have seen the last ____ In the cortage that just has passed ____ They have each filled a page in the annals of time and they're just the same to day. ____

AFTER THE BALL

...As...
Sung by
J. Aldrich
Libbey
...the...
Peerless Baritone
in HOYT'S
"A Trip to
Chinatown"

5

-- BY --
Chas. K. Harris
AUTHOR OF
"...ss and Let's Make Up"

TRADE MARK
CHAS. K. HARRIS

CHICAGO
LYON & HEALY.

Boston
OLIVER DITSON CO.
Philadelphia
J. E. DITSON & CO.
New York
C. H. DITSON & CO.

AFTER THE BALL.

Arr. by JOS. CLAUDER.

Words and Music by CHAS. K. HARRIS.

Tempo di Valse,

1. A   lit - tle maid - - en   climbed an old man's knee...........
2. Bright   lights were flash - - ing   in the grand ball - room,...........
3. Long   years have passed   child,.......... I've nev - er wed,...........

Begged   for a sto - ry- "Do   Un - cle please.".........
Soft   ly the mu - sic,   play - ing sweet tunes.............
True   to my lost   love,   though she is dead...........

Why   are you sin - gle;   why   live   a - lone?...........
There came my sweet - - heart,   my   love,   my own–...........
She   tried to tell   me,   tried   to   ex - plain;........

Have   you   no ba - - - bies;   have   you no   home?........
'I   wish some wa - - - ter;   leave   me a - lone'........
I   would not list - en,   plead - - ings were   vain,.........

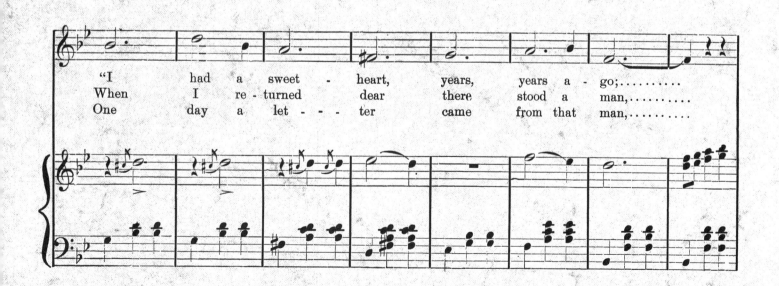

"I   had a sweet - heart,   years,   years a - go;.........
When   I re - turned   dear   there   stood a   man,.........
One   day a let - - ter   came   from that   man,.........

Where she is now pet, you will soon know.........
Kiss - ing my sweet - heart as the lov - ers can.........
He was her broth - er— the let - ter ran.........

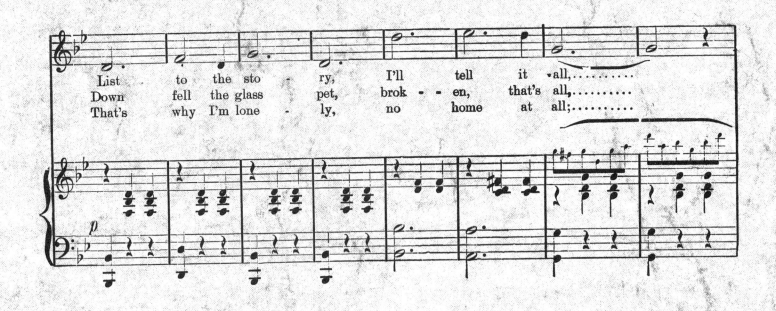

List to the sto - ry, I'll tell it all,..........
Down fell the glass pet, brok - - en, that's all,..........
That's why I'm lone - ly, no home at all;..........

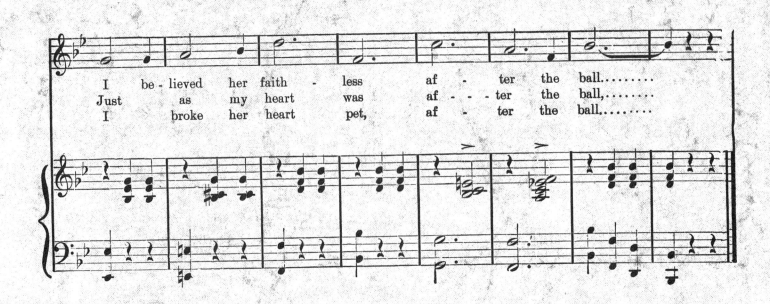

I be - lieved her faith - less af - ter the ball.........
Just as my heart was af - - - ter the ball,.........
I broke her heart pet, af - ter the ball.........

CHORUS.

Af-ter the ball is o - - ver, af-ter the break of morn— Af-ter the dan - cers'

leav - ing; af-ter the stars are gone;........ Many a heart is ach - ing,

if you could read them all;...... Ma- ny the hopes that have van - ished af - - ter the

ball..... ...

D. S.

D.S.

PART THREE

COMIC SONGS & POPULAR NOVELTIES

We Get Up at 8 A. M.

DUET.
Valleda and Leandro.

№ 17.

Allegro moderato.

Piano.

Vall.

1. A maid's ca-reer is skit-tles and beer When she lives in a
2. Our Ann-ual Ball, in the ser- -vants' hall, I'm sure you would de.-

p

Lean.

swell sit-u-a-tion, Noth-ing all day But wait for my pay And
-clare ver-y class-y, We on-ly ask pals, And we don't want gals, Whom the

kiss all the girls in quick ro-ta-tion like
up-stair folk would call *très pas-sé!* like

Both.

For we get up at 8 a. m., 8 a. m.! 8 a. m.! We

break-fast, lun-cheon, tea, and _ dine, Liq - uor and cof-fee at half-past-nine, And

then we dance till late a. m. late a. m.! a. m.! We're

real - ly aw - f'ly bus - y in the ser - vants' hall.

BY THE WRITERS OF "SYMPATHY AND" "GOOD ADVICE"

A FRIEND OF MINE TOLD A FRIEND OF MINE

WORDS BY
ALFRED BRYAN

MUSIC BY
KENDIS & PALEY

COOPER KENDIS & PALEY
MUSIC PUB. CO.
110 WEST 40TH STREET
NEW YORK CITY

5

A Friend Of Mine Told A Friend Of Mine.

Words by
ALFRED BRYAN.

Music by
KENDIS — PALEY

I found a thou-sand dol-lars on the
I want-ed all my friends to make some

street one day___ And tried my ver-y best to keep it
mon-ey too___ The way we'd beat the book-ies was a

mum___ I told it to Eph John-son on the
sin___ My wife told her re-la-tions to bet

street Q. T.___ And Eph he told an-oth-er friend___
all they had___ The tip was eigh-teen kar-at fine___

friend of his__ And he told him not to say a word a-bout it Then that

same friend's friend told an-oth-er friend And the ru-mor spread a

bout ___ Or { And ev-'ry one that told it told the oth-er not to tell }
The preach-er told the sex-ton and the sex-ton tolled the bell } That's the

way they let the se-cret out.___ Well a out.

1.

2.

VOCAL & INSTRUMENTAL NUMBERS.
FROM THE NEW MUSICAL COMEDY

THE ROGERS BROS

"IN LONDON"

Management of   KLAW & ERLANGER.

VOCAL

Mister Breezy Was an Easy Mark	.50
Say You'll Be a Friend of Mine.	.50
Queen of the Bungalow	.50
On a Starlight Night.	.50
American Beauty	.50
You Dream of Me Dear	.50
The Coster's Holiday	.50
By the Sycamore Tree	.50
In Gay New York	.50
It's Awfully Hard to Shop	.50

INSTRUMENTAL

Grand Selection (The Rogers Bros. in London) Piano Solo	1.00
March and Two-step (The Rogers Bros. in London) Piano Solo	.50
Waltz (The Rogers Bros. in London) Piano Solo	.50

SINGING RIGHTS RESERVED.

BOOK BY
J. J. MCNALLY
LYRICS BY
GEORGE V. HOBART
AND
ED. GARDENIER.

MUSIC BY
MAX HOFFMANN &
M. MELVILLE ELLIS

The Rogers Bros Music Pub. Co
NEW YORK THEATRE BUILDING
BROADWAY bet 44th & 45th STS.
NEW YORK.
M WITMARK & SONS London

5

BY THE SYCAMORE TREE.

Words by GEO. V. HOBART.

Music by MAX HOFFMANN.

He's a speak-in' to me,— He said "To whit!"— He
He's a speak-in' to me,— He said "To woo!"— He

said "To woo!"— And that's what I pro - pose to do — And
said "To whit!"— And that's all I can make of it — You

rall. *a tempo* *rall.*

say, sir, who will woo with you By the sy - ca-more tree. The owl said
can't talk owl a lit - tle bit By the sy - ca-more tree. The owl said

CHORUS.
Soft and Slow.

"Woo Sue!" By the sy - ca-more tree, ———— The owl said

"woo do!"_____ And I know he meant me,_____

_____ You're a wise old fowl Close yo' eyes old owl, Don't you

peep at me For you sure-ly see I'll woo my Sue____

_____ By the sy-ca-more tree._____ The owl said

UP IN THE COCOANUT TREE

A. Floyd Featherston

WORDS BY

EDWARD MADDEN

MUSIC BY

THEODORE F. MORSE

Song .... 50c.
Mandolin and Guitar ..... 40c.
Mandolin and Piano ..... 40c.
Banjo and Guitar ..... 40c.
Banjo and Piano ..... 40c.
2 Mandolins and Guitar ..... 50c.
Orchestra 10 parts and Piano .75c.
Orchestra, 14 parts and Piano .95c.
2 Mandolins, Guitar and Piano .6oc.
Mixed Quartette ..... 25c.
Male Quartette ..... 25c.
Mandolin Solo ..... 30c.
Banjo Solo ..... 30c.

ALSO KNOWN AS "THOUGH I AM KING OF THE COCOANUT GROVE" AND "KING OF THE COCOANUT GROVE."

UP IN THE COCOANUT TREE.

Words by EDWARD MADDEN.

Music by THEODORE F. MORSE.

Copyright, MCMIII, by Howley, Haviland & Dresser, New York and Chicago.   English Copyright Secured.

day;.......... He longed for a mate to share his fate,...... 'Mid the grove where he
ways;.......... She thought she would hold the king so bold,...... At her feet ma - ny

held full sway;........ So he spied a lit - tle chim-pan - zee,...... Who
days and days;......... But the wise ba - boon got bu - sy soon,.... For

made her home in a neighb'ring tree;..... And that same night..... when the
on that night, by the light of the moon,.... He swung a - loft...... and

moon shone bright,...... He sang with all his might................
car-ried her off,......... As he sang in ac - cents soft.................

CHORUS.

"Tho' I am King of the co-coa-nut grove I'm lone - ly,.... ... Sweet lit - tle chim pan-

mf–f

zee, I love you on - ly,........ Tho' you are on - ly sweet six - teen, I want you to be my

ba - boon queen, If you'll a - gree you can rule with me, High up in the co-coa-nut tree." "Tho' tree."

1.   2.

8va.

8va.

Geo. Beaverson, 35 Frankfort St., N Y.

And my "Bank" is in the Wabash far away.

Words & Music by H. BOWER.

4

You must pay or move right out, I leave it to you." I
Of-fered in ex-change the girl his hand and his name, In-
Try-ing hard to read a sign on top of the door; "Mo-

real-ly felt em-bar-rassed, what on earth was I to do, His
fact he on-ly mar-ried for he heard his friends de-clare, His
las-ses can-dy Ice-cream, So-da" so his sweet-heart read, But

più mosso.

ang-ry man-ner made me quake with fear,_____ At
Ma'-in-Law was twice a mil-lion-naire,_____ And
he was broke and could not well o-bey,_____ Just

last the song a-bout the "Banks of Wa-bash" met my view, And
when the mar-riage was com-plete he asked her as he smiled, To
then the store-girl came up-on the scene and to him said: "Oh

on the spot it gave me an i - dea! Then I
pay him out the dow - er of her child, But she
treat your girl be-fore you go a - way." He re-

said as I grew ve-ry red: Can - not
said with a shake of her head: Can - not
plied as he drew her a - side: Could - not

CHORUS.

pay you, Must de-lay you, To the Bank I sent my mon - ey just to-

day,____ But don't be fright - ened, When en - light - ened, That my

Bank is in the Wabash far a - way;____ *TUTTI. (All join in the Chorus.)* Can-not pay you, Must de-

ff   *ff*

3. Could-not pay you, Must de-

lay you, To the Bank I sent my mon-ey just to - day,____ But don't be

fright-ened, When en-light-ened, That my Bank is in the Wa-bash far a - way.____

"NAUGHTY DOINGS
ON THE
MIDWAY PLAISANCE"

ONE OF THE GREAT SUCCESSES AS SUNG BY

MARY STUART,
THE CHARMING LITTLE COMEDIENNE.

PUBLISHED BY

WILL ROSSITER,
THE POPULAR SONG PUBLISHER.

MAIN OFFICES, 56 FIFTH AVE., CHICAGO.   Branch, 377 Sixth Ave., New York.

NAUGHTY DOINGS

ON THE MIDWAY PLAISANCE.

Words and Music by W. C. ROBEY.
Arr. by OTTO BONNELL.

INTRODUCTION.
Moderato.

VOICE *Moderato.*

1. I paid a vis - it to the Fair, the wondrous sights to see; I real - ly felt be-
2. The Ja - van - ese, the Ja - pan - ese, the Chi - na - man so gay, Were play - ing on the
3. You'll see the would - be pi - ous girl; she'll take in ev - 'ry show, Then turn un - to her

wil - dered, I con - fess......... Such mar - vel - lous in - ven - tions of in - ge - nu - i - ty; 'Twas
"Tom-tom" loud and strong...... They said it was the music of "Ta - ra - ra - boom - de - aye;" And
friend and say, "Oh, my!"........ She'll say, "Oh, George, you nasty thing, it's wick - ed, that you know;" Then

strange to see the diff'rent styles of dress........ I walked a-bout un-til I saw a
now and then they banged an old cracked gong........ I took a trip to E-gypt, and got
go out-side and "wink the oth - er eye."........ The saint who'd faint to see the legs of

sign that point-ed so, I nudged my friend and gave a know-ing glance..... "He winked his eye" and
on a don-key's back; Their play-ful tricks of course I did-n't know...... His heels went up, and
ta - ble or of stool, Will wait the op-por-tu-ni-ty or chance..... To get in some qui - et

said that he would take me if I'd go, And see the do-ings on Mid-way Plai - sance........
so did mine, they hit him such a whack, Like "Gal-la-gher" they shout-ed, "Let her go!".........
cor - ner there, and take it ver - y cool, Ap-plaud-ing while they do their naught-y dance........

CHORUS. *Marciale.* *2d time allegro.*

On the Mid-way, the Mid-way, the Mid-way Plai-sance, Where the naugh-ty girls from

Al-giers do the "Kou-ta Kou-ta" dance, Mar-ried men when with their wives

give a long-ing glance, At all the naugh-ty do-ings on the Mid-way Plai-sance.

"I Remember You."

"Sung in The Girls of Gottenberg."

Words by
Vincent Bryan.

Music by
Harry Von Tilzer.

av - en - oo?   I re - mem - ber

you, _____   Yes in - deed I do,   Gee! I'm

aw - ful glad I met - cha Bet - cha, life I don't for get - cha I re -

mem - ber   you.   you. _____   D. S.

TELLER, SONS & DORNER.
NEW-YORK.

SUCCESSFULLY · SUNG · BY
GENARO & BAILEY · JOHNSON & DEAN
BEATRICE GOLDEN · · HARRY BROWN
LARKINS & PATTERSON · JOHNNIE HOEY

A · RAGTIME · ODDITY

I · DON'T · SEE · YOUR · NAME
STAMPED · ON · ANY · CIGARS

WORDS BY
SAMUEL · M · LEWIS

MUSIC BY
SAMUEL · PEYSER

THE CHARMING SERIO COMIC
MADGE FOX

L. R. Maltby.

5 4/-

Published by JOS. W. STERN & CO.

I Don't See Your Name Stamped On Any Cigars.

Words by Sam Lewis.

Music by Sam Peyser.

Moderato.

1. Jas - per Boone, a swell dressed loon was tryin' to court a gal named
2. Boone played tricks in pol - i - tics, he was the lead - er of the

lunch;__ She came back to town, Boone called a round, she was the
three:__ On e- -lec -tion day the bands played gay, and Mis-ter

cen -ter of a crowd,__ And as he took a chair, he got the
Boone a-rose to speak,__ But as he start-ed in, the crowd be-

i -cy stare, which made him yell out loud;__
gan to grin, when Belle be -gan to shriek:__

REFRAIN.

I ain't seen a your name__ stamped on a-ny ci -gars.__
I ain't seen a your name__ stamped on a-ny ci -gars.__

p-f

Like the Lil-li-an Rus-sell, Del-la Fox or oth-er stars: Now you
Like the Hen-ry clay, Hen-ry George, and the oth-er po-lit-i-cal stars: Now you

need-n't think, gal-be-cause you're on the stage that you are
say Mis-ter Boone, you're out for states man's fame I think the

go-in' to use me as a will-ing page, Cause I ain't seen-a-your
brand that you're smo king is all to blame, Cause I ain't seen-a-your

name stamped on an-y ci gars.
name stamped on an-y ci gars.

D.S.

OH! I'VE LOST IT.

COMIC SONG and CHORUS

AS SUNG WITH GREAT SUCCESS BY

DAN W. QUINN.

WORDS & MUSIC BY

FELIX McGLENNON.

NEW YORK

Published by HOWLEY, HAVILAND & CO., 4 East 20th St.

5

OH! I'VE LOST IT!

COMIC SONG.

Words by TOM BROWNE.

Music by FELIX McGLENNON.

Allegro Moderato.

3. The
4. They

1. A
2. The

night was dark and gloom-y and the ves-sel pitch'd and lurched— De-
searched with lan-terns till the dawn when all were worn and tired— Then

no-ble yacht was cruis-ing where the seas were roll-ing high A
cap-tain said "What is it Miss? say, have you lost your purse?" "Oh,

CHORUS.

"Oh! I've lost it!" the maid-en fair ex-claimed "Oh! I've lost it! and at home I will be blamed" And then the cap-tain and the crew and the passengers look'd 'round But what the maid-en lost that night could nev-er a-gain be found found

OMAHA IS MY OWN TOWN
J·G·McCRORY CO. 5 AND 10¢ STORE
Schlitz Hotel
Words & Music by DICK B. BRUUN
Sung with GREAT SUCCESS at the EMPRESS GARDEN by
CHORUS—
"TELL ALL THE FOLKS IN OMAHA
THAT I'LL BE BACK SOME DAY,
WHEN I RETURN, I'LL NEVER YEARN
TO LEAVE THERE, BUT I'LL STAY
(RIGHT THERE WHERE)
FOLKS WERE ALWAYS GOOD TO ME,
WHERE FORTUNE SMILES RIGHT DOWN.
IT'S THE BEST OLD PLACE IN THE
UNITED STATES—
OMAHA IS MY OWN TOWN."
MARSHALL & MOORE
5
WALK-OVER SHOE
Photograph by Louis R. Bostwick
Published by the DICK B. BRUUN CO. Omaha
BAKER BROS. ENGRAVERS. OMAHA

"OMAHA IS MY OWN TOWN"

TO THE OMAHA AD. CLUB

Words & Music by
DICK B. BRUUN

Tempo di Marcia

Till ready

Were you ev - er far from home,____ far a - cross the
I can see the sum - mer sun - shine out in Hans - com

sea,_____ In a strange, strange place with not a face to
Park;_____ Thereare peo - ple, too, at Riv - er - view

bring a mem - o - ry of the old home, Un - til   one day there came your
ma - ny   that I   knew in the old days At the Em - press Gar - den bright lights

way   a friend of ___ long a - go, _____ And _ as his ship set
shine, the Pax - ton, the Hen - shaw, the Rome, _____ And the crowd at Six - teenth

sail and he waved you from the   rail   you said, "Tell O - ma - ha." _____
Street, used to know each face I'd   meet   in O - ma - ha, my   home. _____

CHORUS

Tell all the folks in ___ O - ma - ha _____   that I'll be back some

p-f

THE LATEST NEW YORK & LONDON SUCCESS.

"OH! UNCLE JOHN."

Sam F. Goss.

CHORUS.

Oh! Uncle John, isn't it nice on Broadway,
Oh! Uncle John, here I will remain;
Oh! Uncle John, now that I've seen the Bow'ry
Life in the Country's awful slow & I'll never go back again.

COMIC SONG BY FELIX McGLENNON.

SONG ... 40	
Two Step,	40
Guitar,	40
Zither,	25
Two Step, Orch.,	
10 Pts. & Piano,	75
Vocal Orch.,	25
Male Quartette,	25

SUNG WITH THE GREATEST POSSIBLE SUCCESS BY

Miss KITTIE GILMORE,
THE GIFTED COMEDIENNE.

POOR MAIDEN RUTH.

NEW YORK.

Published by SPAULDING & GRAY, 16 W. 27th Street.

FRANCIS, DAY & HUNTER, 198 Oxford St., W. London, England.

DEDICATED TO
CHARLES J. STOCKING, Esq.,
NEW YORK CITY.

OH! UNCLE JOHN.

COMIC SONG.

Words and Music by FELIX McGLENNON.

Moderato.

1. Maid - en Ruth one day came in - to town, Just to see her un - cle dear, ... Maid - en Ruth had on a girl - ish gown,
2. Un - cle John es - cort - ed maid - en Ruth, All a - round the town with care, ... First he took her up to Cen - tral Park,
3. Un - cle some - how lost her in the crowd, Up and down the street he ran, ... Soon he found her hap - py as could be,

And it made her look so queer; . . . . Maid - en Ruth had
Then they went to Chat - ham Square; . . . . Strange sights maid - en
Chat - ting with a po - lice - man, ... Un - cle John then

nev - er seen New York, Not un - til that day poor thing, ...
Ruth had wit-nessed from, Har - lem down to New York bay, ...
said to maid - en Ruth, "Come a - long" but Ruth re - plied, ...

As her un - cle took her all a - round, She be - gan to sing. . .
Ev - 'ry one could tell what pleas'd her most, By the way she'd say. . .
"I must kiss that handsome man in blue," So she did and cried. . .

colla voce.

CHORUS.

LITTLE GERTIE MURPHY

BY HUGHIE CANNON
AUTHOR OF "BILL BAILEY WON'T YOU PLEASE COME HOME."

Arthur Klein

1440 BROADWAY NEW YORK

HOWLEY, DRESSER COMPANY.

Little Gertie Murphy.

INTRODUCTION.
Tempo di Valse.

By HUGHIE CANNON.

I got de beaut lit - tle sweet - heart, She don't tog so
Dis ain't no pipe or no raw - jaw, Goi - tie's got
I'll tell some more a - bout Goi - tie, I tink she is

aw - ful - ly fine, But when we prowl o - ver to
all of de cush, And when we are out wid de
all of de woiks, She hangs out wid Flor - rie and

Joi - sey, De guys dey all tink we're in line, She
wise guys, You know dat we're right in de push, I
Chris - tie, And den butts a - round to Mc - Goiks, She's

ain't got a face like a freight-train, Wid me she's a
ain't got to do no more prowl-ing, She al-ways treats
loin-ing to be a fine goil-ie, In danc-ing she's

might-y swell dame, Her dad and her mud-der are
me just the same, I can't e-ven smoke a brain
got all de twoils, She just goes a-round wid her

I - rish, Its eas'-ly to tell by her name.
cap - sule, When I'm wid dis lit-tle dame.
Mick - ey And don't lal - a gagg wid de goils.

CHORUS.

Lit - tle Goi - tie Moi - phy, boys, I tell you she's a

boid, She lives on thoi - ty - sec - ond street, Next to

thoi - ty - thoid, And she buys de New York Joi - nal, And she

reads de Sun - day Woild, And I'm proud of Goi - tie Moi - phy,

When her hair is coiled. coiled.

SO LONG MARY

SONG SUCCESSES FROM

GEO. M COHAN'S

LATEST MUSICAL PLAY
≈ PLAYED BY ≈
FAY TEMPLETON
UNDER THE DIRECTION OF
KLAW & ERLANGER

FORTY-FIVE MINUTES FROM BROADWAY

SONGS *of the* PLAY

1. RETIRING FROM THE STAGE
2. I WANT TO BE A POPULAR MILLIONAIRE
3. MARY'S A GRAND OLD NAME
4. FORTY-FIVE MINUTES FROM BROADWAY
5. STAND UP AND FIGHT LIKE HELL
6. SO LONG MARY

5

PUBLISHED BY F.A.MILLS. 48 WEST 29TH ST., NEW YORK.

Public performance prohibited without permission.

"So Long Mary."

GEO. M. COHAN.

"It's awf-'ly nice of all you girls to
"It's awf-'ly kind of all you boys to

see me to the train." "So long, Ma - ry." "I
see me off to - day." "So long, Ma - ry." "I

CHORUS.

did - n't think you'd care if you should ne'er see me a - gain."
did - n't think you'd care if I should eith - er go or stay."

CHORUS.

"You're wrong, Ma - ry." "This re - minds me of my fam - i - ly,
"You're wrong, Ma - ry." "Yes, I'm going to oth - er lands to dwell,

On the day I left Sche - nec - ta - dy, To the de - pot
Awf - 'ly nice of you to wish me well; Hard - ly thought a

then they came with me— I seem to hear them say:"
soul in New Ro - chelle would ev - en come to say:"

CHORUS.

"So long, Ma ry; Ma - ry, we will miss you

TOMMY WAS A BAD. BAD. BAD. BOY

WORDS & MUSIC BY

PAUL ARMSTRONG

5

PUBLISHED BY
HOWLEY, HAVILAND & DRESSER
1260 1266 BROADWAY,
NEW YORK

Starmer

TOMMY WAS A BAD, BAD BOY.

COMIC SONG.

Words & Music by PAUL ARMSTRONG.

A big black pipe was ly - ing on the shelf, Tom-my was a bad, bad
His ma she found him doubled up with pain, Tom-my was a bad, bad
He died quite young or he'd be liv - ing yet Tom-my was a bad, bad

boy, _____ He wink'd his eye and then he hump'd his self,
boy, _____ She tried to ques - tion him but all in vain,
boy, _____ Went swim - ming Sun - day and his feet got wet,

Tom-my was a bad, bad boy, _____ Took a match and
Tom-my was a bad, bad boy, _____ In des-pair she
Tom-my was a bad, bad boy, _____ 'Neath a stone that

then he struck a light, Sat him down to smoke with all his might,
sought the tel-e-phone, Called the Doc and asked him if he'd come,
tells a sto-ry well, Says he's gone to Heav-en there to dwell,

Soon he was in an aw-ful plight! Tom-my was a bad, bad boy.
Came with a stomach pump used it some! Tom-my was a bad, bad boy.
Can't most al - - ways some times tell! Tom-my was a bad, bad boy.

REFRAIN.

Oh my! why should he be born, Just to make his fam-i-ly for-lorn,

Tales too sad, I can't go on, Tom-my was a bad, bad boy.

Dance *ad lib.*

Extra Verses.

1.

A great big circus came to town one day,
    Tommy was a bad, bad boy.
Kept hangin' 'round and couldn't keep away,
    Tommy was a bad, bad boy.
Watched his chance, and underneath he went
Found himself in the ladies dressing tent
If they hadn't thrown him out he'd be there yet
    Tommy was a bad, bad boy.
Chorus. Oh my! why should he be born,
    Just to make his family forlorn,
    Tales too sad I can't go on,
    Tommy was a bad, bad boy.

2.

His sister's Cholly came to call one night,
    Tommy was a bad, bad boy.
Beneath the sofa he was out of sight,
    Tommy was a bad, bad boy.
The light went out as sometimes it will do
The kid was wise and knew a thing or two
H'm .... a few,
    Tommy was a bad, bad boy.
Chorus Great Scott, the kid is flying high
    Money to burn and eats all kinds of pie
    Got it all from Cholly and he won't tell why
    Tommy was a bad, bad boy.

3.

The first typewriter that he ever saw
    Tommy was a bad, bad boy.
Was in the office of his brother-in-law
    Tommy was a bad, bad boy.
"Say ma" says he "do they put wine in this?"
"Why no" said she "what foolishness this is!"
"Well pa said he poured three quarts in his!"
    Tommy was a bad, bad boy.
Chorus. Oh my! why should he be born, &c.

4.

He went to Sunday school as all boys should
    Tommy was a bad, bad boy.
He tried real hard to be so sweet and good
    Tommy was a bad, bad boy.
Teacher said "come Tommy let us see
If you cant tell who made both you and me"
"Aint biting at any old gags" says he
    Tommy was a bad, bad boy.
Chorus. Oh my! why should he be born, &c.

Look Out for Him!

"McCLOSKEY ON THE SPREE"

Comic Irish Song and Chorus.

WORDS AND MUSIC BY

J. P. SKELLY.

PUBLISHED BY

WILL ROSSITER,

204 DEARBORN STREET,

CHICAGO.

"McCLOSKEY ON THE SPREE."

Words and Music by

J. P. SKELLY.

Piano.

1. When on his "Pe - ri - od - i - cals" Mc-Clos-key is a fright, To
2. He goes in - to the cor - ner where The mug-wumps con - gre-gate, And
3. Al-though he is a la - dies' man, When so - ber and se - rene, The
4. He quar - rels with O'-Hoo - li - gan, Mc-Fad - den and Mc-Ginn, With

Have you got the beautiful song, "Life is too Short, to Worry or Fret?" A true to life story.

ag - gra - vate the neigh - bors, seems to be his sole de - light; He
shouts a loud de - fi - ance, till he's told to "take a skate;" With
vis - ion of a wom - an, fills him with a woe - ful spleen, They
Of - fi - cer O' - Reil - ly and his cro - ny, Mick - ey Flynn, But

wants to own the side - walk, and The house and fam - i - ly, You'll
an - y one and ev - 'ry one, He's bound to dis - a - gree, They
fly from him in ter - ror when His scowl - ing face they see, They
with a wise phil - os - o - phy They one and all a - gree, To

hear the boys all shout - ing, "There's Mc - Clos - key on the spree."
say its hu - man dy - na - mite, Mc - Clos - key on the spree.
know he's "got them on him," its Mc - Clos - key on the spree.
down their woes to - geth - er with Mc - Clos - key on the spree.

The latest hit in waltz songs, "LITTLE NORA MALONE."

CHORUS. *Con Forza.*

He pounds up-on the ta-ble with a bang, bang, bang, He cries, "come out, Mc-Car-thy, and your gang, gang, gang," He dan-ces in the hall-way, And he laughs a fiend-ish glee, The talk of all the neigh-bors is, "Mc-Clos-key on the spree."

The second edition of "**Cute little Shoes and Stockings**" is now ready.

THE WAY TO ASK A GIRL TO MARRY.

Words by
RAYMOND A. BROWNE.
Author of "The way to kiss a girl."

Music by
LEO FRIEDMAN.
Composer of "Memories of the south."

Moderato.

If per-chance you love a pret-ty maid-en
She may hes-i-tate be-fore she an-swers:

One you'd like to make your wife some day,
Blush-ing like a rose be-fore she'll speak;

And you dont know how to go and ask her
But shes not to blame be-cause pro-po-sals

List-en, and I'll tell to you the way:
Are not things that hap-pen ev-'ry day,

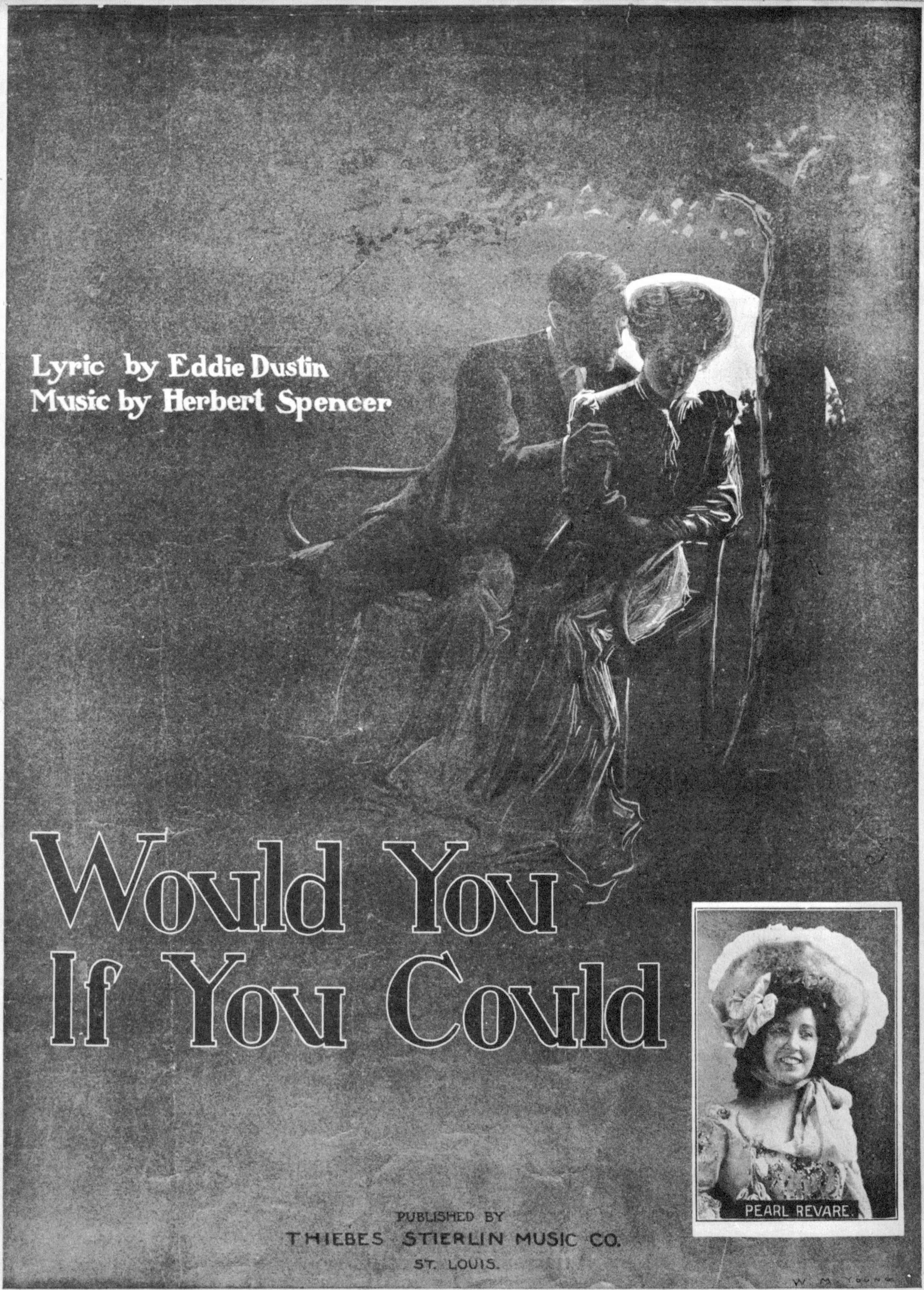
Lyric by Eddie Dustin
Music by Herbert Spencer
Would You If You Could
PEARL REVARE.
PUBLISHED BY
THIEBES STIERLIN MUSIC CO.
ST. LOUIS.
W. M. YOUNG

WOULD YOU IF YOU COULD.

Words by
EDDIE DUSTIN.

Music by
HERBERT SPENCER

Moderato.

1. Have you ev_er wooed a maid_en
2. If for ev_ery shoot_ing star the

on a sum_mers eve_ning When the stars shone bright
maid would let you kiss her And al_low some hugs

Shad_ows dart_ing here and there You won_der if she'd real_ly care To
Would you treat the maid_en square Keep your glanc_es in the air And

hear your lit—tle tale of love to—night
not go ring—ing in the light—ning bugs

When the maid—en seems so shy you think 'tis such a pi—ty as you
Should the maid—en ask you if you have an—oth—er sweet—heart would you

hold her hand Tho' your heart with love is mel—low she's a
an—swer "No" Vow by all the stars a—bove her

girl and you're a fel—low How are you to ev—er ev—er un—der—stand!
That you ve—ry mad—ly love her He who he—si—tates is lost you know.

CHORUS.

Would you if you could Could you if she would

Stand for just a kiss per _ haps a lit _ tle hug so good

If she'd say "oh dear" Some one may be near

Could you mur _ mur "dar _ ling nev _ er fear"

INDEX OF SONGS

INDEX OF FIRST LINES

NORTON STILLMAN started collecting old sheet music almost by accident. As his collection grew, it brought back many happy memories. . . . When he was a boy in Minneapolis, his family frequently got together at Grandma Grace and Grandpa Harry's house down the street. Aunt Marian played the piano and sang. Uncle Arthur joined in and Uncle George accompanied them on his violin. Norton's dad sang, too— and even broke into a yodel at certain choruses! Then there was Uncle Leonard—he couldn't carry a tune, but when the song was lively, he snapped his fingers in time to the music. . . .

You'll have a finger-snapping good time, too, with *Trust Me With Your Heart Again.*